GROWING OLD IN SILENCE

Growing Old in Silence

GAYLENE BECKER

University of California Press

Berkeley / Los Angeles / London

University of California Press
Berkeley and Los Angeles, California

University of California Press, Ltd.
London, England

© 1980
The Regents of the University of California

1 2 3 4 5 6 7 8 9

Library of Congress Cataloging in Publication Data

Becker, Gaylene.
    Growing old in silence.

    Bibliography: p.
    Includes index.
    1. Aged, Deaf. 2. Aging. I. Title.
HV2395.B4   362.4'2'0880565   79-63548
ISBN 0-520-03900-9

For Roger

Contents

Preface

During the process of collecting information for a research project in community mental health, I was invited to attend the organizational meeting of a group of elderly deaf people, sponsored by a local agency. I knew little sign language at that time, but I decided to go, out of curiosity. It was a moving experience. Although I understood little of what was actually said that day, the shouts of joy and laughter as a hundred people swarmed into the room and were reunited with each other were easy for me to interpret.

Long after the meeting was over, the spectacle that I had witnessed remained in my mind. I began to think about the meaning of growing old, about the kinds of life experiences that people have, and about how these experiences affect old age. In particular, I began to ask myself questions. How were these deaf individuals different from my own "hearing" grandparents and from other aged persons? How were they the same? But most of all, I wondered how they could appear to function so well in the face of such a severe disability. My interest captured, I ultimately returned to the scene of my first encounter to learn more.

I received considerable support from several federal agencies during the research and writing of the manuscript: National Institute on Aging grant AG-00022 (formerly HD-00238,

National Institute of Child Health and Human Development), and Administration on Aging Training Grant 90-A-1195(01). Chapter eleven was written during the time I was funded by a National Science Foundation Postdoctoral Fellowship, SM177-12424. The funding has played an important role in the completion of this study, and I hope the federal government will continue to lend its support to social science research.

This study was an exercise in applied anthropology. Its purpose was to provide anthropological perspectives on the aged deaf for practitioners who provide services to disabled populations, and consequently many individuals have participated in this process. I am especially indebted to Margaret Clark who encouraged me to study the aged deaf. The opportunity to work with her and to benefit from her brilliant insights into human behavior has been invaluable to me. I am grateful to Joan Ablon, an inspired teacher, who has imparted her philosophy about applied anthropology to me over the years and has given me the training to carry out such a study. George Foster has made thoughtful comments and suggestions that have been extremely valuable during the writing process. In addition, I want to thank Clifford Barnett, Sharon Kaufman, and James Spradley for their criticisms and suggestions.

A number of professionals who work with the deaf community have shared their insights about deafness with me, and a few have read and criticized portions of this work. I especially want to thank Rhoda Clark, Gay Nadler, Jacqueline Hynes Peterson, and Connie Yannacone. I am grateful to John Darby of the Hearing Society of San Francisco for introducing me to the aged deaf, and to Kathryn P. Meadow and Hilde S. Schlesinger of the University of California Center on Deafness for giving me access to classes and materials related to deafness. My special thanks go to Kristine Bertelsen, who criticized the manuscript, made editorial suggestions, and typed most of it as well.

Roger Van Craeynest has been a source of continual support

over the years as this study evolved. His understanding of the complexities of deafness and its anthropological implications has been invaluable, as have his criticisms and ideas throughout the research and writing.

Most of all, I wish to thank the older members of the deaf community. The anthropologist who receives the full cooperation of the people he or she studies is fortunate indeed. People generously gave me their time and their friendship, and I am grateful for their willingness to teach me their language and introduce me to their culture. Naturally, I alone am responsible for the content and interpretations found in the text.

Many informants expressed a wish that their individual life experiences might have some relevance for future generations of deaf people. I hope that they will view my interpretation of those experiences as consistent with that goal.

I

Entering the Community

Singer raised his hands timidly and began to speak. His strong, skilled fingers shaped the signs with loving precision. He spoke of the cold and of the long months alone. He mentioned old memories, the cat that had died, the store, the place where he lived. At each pause Antonapoulos nodded graciously. . . . Eagerly Singer leaned closer. . . .

CARSON McCULLERS, *The Heart Is a Lonely Hunter* (1940:187–188)

I first saw Stella Jackson at a special workshop for older deaf people.[1] She immediately caught my eye as she made her way through a crowded room, pausing to greet each person enthusiastically. An attractive seventy-year-old woman, Mrs. Jackson was wearing a checked shirtwaist dress with a big bow tie. She was small and slender, with short gray hair, curled in a casual style. She radiated vitality and warmth; people flocked around her, hugging her and exchanging small talk with her. As I watched Mrs. Jackson and her friends I saw none of the symptoms of self-hatred, denial, and depression so commonly described in the gerontological literature.

Many hearing people in the general population are vigorous

1. Pseudonyms are used throughout the text to preserve anonymity. In addition, details of individuals' lives have been altered to render them totally unrecognizable—for example, occupation, family size, school ties, and other identifying factors.

and well-adapted in old age. Perhaps the deaf are not more well-adjusted than their hearing contemporaries. But most hearing people have not been excluded from major American institutions, such as public schools, over the life-span, as have the deaf. It seemed logical to me that lifelong exclusion would have a negative influence on adjustment to life, and it came as a surprise when I observed the high degree of social intactness among these aging deaf people.

When I introduced myself to Mrs. Jackson she was very friendly. She made every effort to communicate with me, slowing down the speed of her signs and finger-spelling, and articulating carefully. She was interested in learning about me as a student, and she established me in relation to her own social world by asking me about my sign language teachers and about mutual acquaintances. She was open to talking about herself too, and over the course of the following year she told me much about her life.

Mrs. Jackson's adjustment to old age as a deaf person is exemplary. In fact, Mrs. Jackson's warm social personality struck me from the beginning of our acquaintance. Yet her life had not been a happy and painless one. As I talked with her I was struck repeatedly by the ways in which she had learned to deal with her deafness.

Mrs. Jackson slowly and painfully learned to cope with her deafness, beginning in her earliest years. "Being deaf has been hard," she says. Her mother never learned sign language and thus could not communicate with her except through gestures and writing. This was particularly difficult for her in a family that, as she says, "always put a lot of stock in family togetherness . . . because I'm deaf I have always been an outsider." [2]

It was as an outsider that she left home when she was five years old to attend a state school for the deaf. There she dis-

2. American Sign Language does not conform to the grammatical and syntactical structure of English. Therefore, I have translated informants' comments into English wherever appropriate.

covered a new world. For the first time she learned the signs for words. She could communicate not only with the teacher but with other children as well. Predictably, Mrs. Jackson loved school and hated to go home in the summertime, where silence once again closed in around her.

For over twelve years Mrs. Jackson stayed in the state school. The environment, which had initially seemed so exciting, grew restricting. Curious about the outside world, she struck out on her own when she was seventeen, eager to experience independence.

Lacking job skills, Mrs. Jackson had a hard time finding work. When she finally did get a job in a factory, she was fortunate to find another deaf woman, Mabel Griggs, working there. Mabel's presence made the grueling work of the assembly line bearable. They became close friends, a relationship that has continued to the present.

"It was an exciting time of life," says Mrs. Jackson, "making my own money, doing what I wanted." She and Mabel shared an apartment, and on the weekends they went to the deaf club, to picnics, and to sports events sponsored by different groups in the deaf community. Mrs. Jackson met her husband-to-be at one of these picnics some five years after leaving school. He had recently arrived from the Midwest. Like Mrs. Jackson, he had gone to a state school for the deaf. Six months later they were married.

At first, married life was enjoyable. They had plenty of friends and led a busy social life. Mrs. Jackson had to stop working when their first child was born, but they could not live on her husband's salary (he was a printer's apprentice), so she had to go back to work at the factory. "It seemed like overnight we started to fight about everything. We couldn't get along." But they continued to live together, Mrs. Jackson always hoping things would get better. "Being deaf, I didn't know the first thing about getting a divorce. I didn't see any way out."

Soon after their second child was born her husband was laid off, and the economic strain brought a sudden end to their married life. They split up, Mrs. Jackson taking her two hearing children home for her mother to take care of, and going back to the factory to earn money for their support. Her husband left the area in search of work, and her family eventually helped her obtain a divorce. "That was a bad time. When I was young, divorce was not common, and some of the people in the deaf community looked down on me. My kids didn't like it much either, but I think they understand better now that they're grown. My relationship with my son is better. Now he does occasional interpreting, [and] we have more to talk about."

One Saturday evening at the deaf club a visitor walked in, a deaf man from New York who was moving to San Francisco. He and Mrs. Jackson got along from the start. Fifteen years had passed since her divorce. Shortly after they met they were married. The tenor of Mrs. Jackson's life changed dramatically with her remarriage. For the first time since she left school money ceased to be a source of stress. Her second husband was a glazier with a comfortable income. "Oh, what a relief! I was finally able to leave that awful factory." Since that time she has enjoyed being a housewife.

Mr. Jackson has considerable prestige in the community. Mrs. Jackson, after many years as "a divorcee," enjoys the social standing she has acquired as a respectably married woman. The end of her drudgery and her heightened status in the community have enhanced her relationship with her husband. They do everything together except watch television. Television is really important to Mrs. Jackson because it is her link with the outside world. She watches all captioned TV programs, and as these programs have increased in number they have begun to conflict with her husband's sports viewing. Finally, he went out and bought her a TV of her own. She is very happy about it. "One of the hardest things about being deaf is not knowing what's going on in the world. I felt shut out for so long." According to her, her ideal day includes staying home and reading, knitting, and watching television. "Some deaf go to socials all the time, but twice a week is enough for me."

Mr. and Mrs. Jackson are active in the social life of their peer group. They no longer go to the deaf club, because they do not like to go out at night. Instead, they go to senior citizen groups and alumni meetings. They spend a lot of time visiting with friends, often meeting them at the various functions they attend. Mrs. Jackson now calls up her friends on her newly acquired TTY (a teletypewriter attached to a telephone) when she wants to see or talk to them. She contrasts the easy way of communicating with people with what she did in the past. Now she can make plans a day or so in advance, instead of waiting until the next deaf social to make all her plans at once. Even better, if she needs to cancel an appointment she can use her TTY instead of leaving the person waiting and wondering what happened to her. Mrs. Jackson says, "You know, being deaf sets you apart. Not being able to use a phone, having to carry around a pad and pencil to write with, and knowing people think you are different . . . it used to bother me a lot, and I guess it still does. I would rather be hearing."

As Mrs. Jackson reviews her life her deafness recurs again and again, as something that has interfered with the smooth flow of daily life. I shall discuss the themes that emerged in her account of her life history later.

Deafness, as I shall use the term, refers to a permanent hearing loss that occurred at birth or in early childhood and prevents an individual from communicating meaningfully through speech. Deafness hinders the development of language and communication skills and thus inhibits the deaf person's social growth and development. Throughout life the deaf individual must make enormous adjustments in order to function in a "hearing" world.[3]

GROWING OLD DEAF

Little is known of how people adapt to deafness over the course of a lifetime. Schlesinger and Meadow (1972:29), who have specialized in mental health issues surrounding deafness, state, "We simply do not know the effect that deafness has on the crisis of old age."

My major thesis in this study is that the ways in which an individual learns to cope early in life with a marginal social status provide him or her with an invaluable repertoire of skills and resources for dealing with the problems encountered in old age. Given the right conditions, disabled populations have the potential for such adaptive behavior, and adaptive strategies, once patterned within a group of such people, contribute in turn to cultural variation. This developmental process takes a lifetime and thus is most apparent from the vantage point of old age. What I have observed is the end of such a process among deaf people who are now old.

Much of the deaf experience is embedded in the fabric of American life. There are, however, significant experiential differences between deaf and hearing people who are the same age. These differences pervade individuals' lives, coloring them and invoking variations in the pattern of life. The key to these variations lies in the progression of adaptive behaviors in each individual's life history, layer building on layer as the individual matures and grows old.

The old individual is the sum of his or her life experience, and views ongoing events in the light of that past experience. This process shapes the individual's world view and influences his or her actions. By the time a person is old this process

3. Hearing loss that occurs in adulthood or later life is not dealt with.

is further influenced by the cumulative effect of long-term adaptive strategies. For example, long before she became old, Mrs. Jackson's friends became a crucial part of the coping mechanisms she developed to deal with different living situations. In fact, peer support became an important part of her life when she was sent to school some seventy years earlier.

In order to understand how the old deaf person functions in daily life, we must examine these formative processes and their influence on the individual. Some of these experiences, such as education, differ radically from that of most Americans, while other experiences, such as marriage, seem no different. The similarities are as crucial as the differences to our understanding of the social patterns that have developed. It is the particular combination of these experiences that contributes to adaptation in old age. Most important, these aging deaf people have demonstrated the ability to transcend some of the differences that exist between them and the outside world and to make their way in American life, a factor that has great implications for their well-being in old age. In chapters two through five I pay considerable attention to the critical life experiences of childhood and young adulthood.

The functioning of deaf people in old age is directly related to their disability. Throughout their lives they have striven to adapt so that they, and their disability, will fit into society. The ways in which they have adjusted to the disability over the course of their lives happen to be particularly adaptive for old age. The behavior of individuals in old age is the final step in a lifelong process of adjustment to deafness and its social consequences. This adjustment begins early in life, at the time language acquisition begins, and continues over the life-span until death. Some of the themes that emerge in the portrait of Mrs. Jackson, such as the continual confrontations with one's disability, play central roles in the adaptive process. The pattern of adaptation to the disability has eased the later adjustment to old age, as will be seen in chapters six through ten.

As we trace the lives of deaf individuals through life histories we shall see how identity is formed and maintained, and how it operates to prepare deaf people for old age. Maintenance of identity among the deaf is reinforced by interaction with the world around them, a world that presumes all its inhabitants can hear.

While development is taking place on a personal level, change is occurring at a cultural level. The idiosyncratic movement of the individual through time interacts with the tide of culture. The interplay between the individual life history and the formation of the group meshes to create a unique subsociety. I have tried to depict this interaction throughout, picking out the various motifs that form pictures of aging deaf people in their cultural context.

Much of the deaf individual's response to disability in relation to identity, personal development, and life adjustment can be explained by social roles and relationships. Therefore, I emphasize the role of social interaction in various contexts throughout the book.

One of the major problems deaf persons face throughout life is the effect that their relationships with others have on their self-esteem. During the course of my fieldwork I saw a pattern in the interaction of the aged deaf recurring again and again. When individuals were in a group of deaf people they were talkative, confident, outgoing and relaxed. When they were interacting with people with normal hearing, whether alone or with only a few deaf people present, they became quiet and hesitant. Strained interaction such as this is not unique; in all societies where different linguistic groups live in close proximity, lack of a common language creates social boundaries (Ross, 1975). Strained interaction is especially frequent in interactions between hearing and deaf people.

Deafness is called an invisible handicap because it is noticeable only when a person attempts to communicate (Meadow,

1976). No visible indicators, such as the white cane of the blind person, give other people cues about what to expect in communication with a deaf person. Once the disability is known, the effect of it may be heightened (Davis, 1961). Hearing people often "freeze" and withdraw from the situation or behave inappropriately. This type of behavior is so common that Schlesinger and Meadow (1972:19) have labeled it "shock withdrawal paralysis." Communication difficulties with hearing people continually arise and always carry the threat of social isolation.

A more subtle problem in social interaction with hearing people results from the discrepancy in social knowledge. Much of what people with normal hearing learn is based on what they overhear (Yambert and Van Craeynest, 1975). This applies most significantly to social knowledge; for example, when children listen to their mothers discussing someone else's behavior, it helps them learn about cultural norms and expectations about behavior. The deaf person, lacking this kind of social knowledge, frequently says things that are inappropriate to common American social interaction. For example, I was sitting in a circle of women at a deaf social. The lady across from me asked me where I went to school. When I responded, "U.C.," she said, "Oh, Mrs. Jones here (indicating the woman next to her) went to U.C. to see a psychiatrist who knew sign language. The doctor helped her a lot. She had bad problems." Mrs. Jones joined in with, "Yes, it was really helpful. I'm much better now." Similar comments by deaf people have been interpreted as shallow, impulsive, emotionally immature, and suggestible (Levine, 1958).

When intercultural communication with the larger social world becomes difficult for any group of people with sufficient numbers to form its own small society, the likelihood is great that the group will rely on its own members to meet most of the social and emotional needs of life. Such is the case with deaf people. They consciously develop a social world that will avoid the complexities of intercultural communication.

FIELD METHODS

In studying the aging process among people already old, I have chosen to view trends over the life course and significant personal events phenomenologically; that is, I have drawn upon the individual's own sense of how his or her life fits together (Hallowell, 1955:79–80). The Great Depression of the 1930s, for example, means different things to different people. Of three deaf men, one man attributes his economic troubles at that time to his deafness, another man cites being an "Okie" for his economic problems, while a third man states that the Depression had no personal significance for him. The uniqueness of an individual's perspective lies in these varied events and the way the individual interprets them. This phenomenological perspective underlies the fieldwork.

I conducted the fieldwork over the course of one year, 1976, using American Sign Language as a means of communication. Traditional anthropological field techniques were used, including participant-observation and interviewing. I first entered into the social life of the people by attending monthly socials for the aged deaf, which took place in an agency's meeting hall. These meetings are held regularly. Hearing visitors are tolerated; they are welcomed once they show an ongoing interest in the group and can communicate easily in sign language.

The development of trust was a slow process. After several months of regular attendance at various socials, I suddenly became very popular. Once people thought my interest was genuine, they began issuing invitations to small parties, luncheons, and large public events. From that time on, I participated as much as possible in the life of the community.

During the course of one year I had contact with aging deaf

people almost daily. I visited people in their homes, and went to luncheons, picnics, fashion shows, public lectures, church services, banquets, and funerals. I drove people to appointments and to social functions and observed them in their daily routines. In the course of my participant-observation I had ample opportunity to observe their relationships with each other, as well as their behavior toward their children, siblings, and neighbors. I observed their interactions with hearing strangers, and was occasionally recruited to aid in communication in these encounters.

I had initially planned to use an interpreter with some informants who had difficulty communicating with me or with whom I had difficulty communicating. This plan soon proved unfeasible when I realized that a person's sense of privacy might be jeopardized by having an interpreter present. As my time in the field passed, my knowledge and understanding of the language improved, and I dispensed with plans to use an interpreter.

Privacy is difficult to maintain in the deaf community because sign language is a public language (Meadow, 1972) that can be seen and understood at some distance. This factor, coupled with an extensive grapevine that keeps people abreast of gossip and news, makes most information public. During the course of my fieldwork I explained the concept of confidentiality to many people. The idea that things people told me would not be passed on to others was foreign to some of them. As time passed, most people understood that I would not repeat anything they told me.

Data were collected from a sample of 200 aging deaf people and from approximately 30 others who were relatives of people in the sample or professionals providing services to the study population. From the sample of 200 a subsample of 60 people was chosen for systematic interviewing.

People in the subsample were chosen from a variety of locales in the San Francisco Bay Area. They represent a range of educational, occupational, and economic backgrounds. Conversations with professionals dealing with deaf individuals from all walks of life convince me that they are typical of the aged deaf in the San Francisco Bay Area.

I chose the age of sixty rather than sixty-five as the cut-off age for the subsample for two reasons. First, it forms a natural division in the deaf community. People begin to attend socials for older people when they are about sixty. Second, I wanted to incorporate some people in my subsample who still worked, so that I could learn about the transition to retirement among this group.

Interviews were semistructured and open-ended. Because of the necessity of establishing the circumstances of each person's hearing loss in order to understand the subsequent events of their lives, I started all initial interviews with questions related to their birth. People usually proceeded to talk about their lives in a chronological way; during their narrative I would interrupt to ask specific questions. During a second interview I would raise issues related to subjects they had mentioned in the previous interview. Of the subsample of 60 persons 20 were formally interviewed two or more times for a period of three to four hours each, 20 people were formally interviewed during one visit, and 20 were informally interviewed in brief sessions, and information was gathered from all 60 during the course of various conversations throughout the year.

The necessity of face-to-face interaction made it impossible for me to write while a person was talking to me. I tried to schedule fieldwork so that I could write notes up immediately after each encounter.

Although I chose 60 people for my subsample, I gathered considerable data about social patterns and life experiences from the other 140 aged deaf people with whom I met and talked. This process was made easier by the importance deaf people attach to oral history and storytelling.

Most people understood that I was an anthropology student, that I wanted to learn about them, and that I would eventually write about them in order to get a degree from the university. Once I was accepted, however, I found that people had their own motives for assisting me. They began to teach me their language and their culture so that I would become their advocate. The philosophy underlying this behavior is that deaf people need the assistance of hearing people who are educated about deafness. Some people think in terms of concrete assistance, such as interpreting an order in a restaurant. Others think of developing skilled interpreters who will be their funnels to the hearing world. Still others think of tertiary prevention, educating the outside world to understand the complexities of deafness through people with normal hearing. The effort to educate me opened doors closed to others; for example, groups of men would admit me, the only woman, to their discussions, on the basis that it would help me learn the language.

When I began my research I wondered if my informants' concern with the problems that surrounded them in childhood would have subsided. I found, however, that they continue to think about and discuss these problems in an effort to come to terms with their experiences as deaf people. Consequently, a large quantity of retrospective data were collected during the fieldwork. Accounts of early life experiences were given with a degree of emotionality not present in any other area of the data collection. The retrospective data, despite the colorations and changed perceptions of time, help to sum up the deaf experience.

The crisis posed by deafness in early childhood does not fade into obscurity with age. Instead, it remains the crux of life, the vantage point from which all other experience is viewed.

III

A Profile of the Aged Deaf

The aged deaf population in the United States is only a small proportion of the general population of old people. At present there are more than 20 million people in the United States over the age of sixty-five (Butler, 1976:xi). In comparison, a recent census of the deaf population of the United States reports that there are approximately 119,000 deaf people over the age of sixty-five (Schein and Delk, 1974:28); this figure includes all people who lost their hearing before the age of eighteen. No breakdown is available for those people who lost their hearing in the first few years of life.

In the San Francisco Bay Area, the only figures available on deaf people over the age of sixty-five are those compiled by organizations serving the deaf aged and by myself. Approximately two hundred older people who are known to the organizations participate in social activities. I estimate that this group represents roughly two-thirds of the deaf people over the age of sixty in the San Francisco Bay Area. Deaf people not included are (1) blacks, who are excluded because of prejudice against them from participation in the activities of this primarily white group and have consequently formed their own social circles; (2) those who do not associate with other deaf people—this category includes individuals whose language skills enable them to socialize easily with hearing people, as well as a small number of social isolates whose communication skills are poor; (3) those who do not affiliate with organizations serving old people. It should be noted, however, that these latter individuals are active in the deaf community in age-integrated organizations. Organizational participation is a way of life among deaf people, and in this regard the sample is extremely representative.

The aged deaf in this study are not necessarily characteristic of other groups of aged deaf in the United States. These individuals share many characteristics common to the deaf experience, such as economic and educational background, but have specific cultural characteristics unique to the sample.

In the Bay Area the population from which the sample was obtained spans five counties: San Francisco, Alameda, Contra Costa, Marin, and San Mateo, with the greatest concentration of deaf people in the cities of Oakland and San Francisco.

The subsample was chosen on the basis of a variety of factors, such as age at hearing loss, present age, sex, educational background, and type of communication skills. The subsample is composed of 60 persons, of whom 34 are women and 26 are men. The mean age of both men and women in the subsample is seventy. The majority of subjects are white, Euro-American ethnically, and middle class. Ninety-two percent of the subsample have been married; of that number, 65 percent were married at the time of the research.

Old deaf people are dispersed throughout the urban area. They live in working-class and middle-class neighborhoods. Two-thirds of the subsample now own their own homes or have owned homes in the past. At the time of the study one-half of the subsample lived in single-family dwellings, and one-half lived in apartments. Half of the apartment dwellers lived in senior housing.

While most of the subsample stayed in school until they were eighteen years old, only about two-thirds graduated from high school. The discrepancy arises because of the difficulty people experienced in mastering English, which in turn affected their ability to perform academically.[1] Of the eight people in the subsample who attended college (13 percent), all but one went to Gallaudet College, the liberal arts college for the deaf in Washington, D.C.

The most common type of work done by nonprofessional deaf men is skilled labor, particularly and traditionally as printers. Seven of twenty-six men in the subsample are printers. Other occupations included carpenter, shoe repairman, machinist, glazier, and clerk. The three professional men were employed as teachers and counselors in schools for the deaf.

Homemaking is the traditional role of older deaf women, as it is with their hearing contemporaries. Nevertheless, almost one-half of the women in the subsample worked outside the home during most of their adult lives. Of 34 women 19 were housewives and 15 were in the work force, as skilled and unskilled laborers, white-collar workers, and professionals. Most working women were married during their working life; however, few of these women had children.

Disabled people without college educations have traditionally had a problem finding employment. The economic limitations resulting from poor job availability for deaf people have had a strong influence on the development of social patterns. Together with educational and communication limitations, these economic considerations have limited the realization of individual potential in the outside world. Individual energies have been rechanneled into building a strong community of the deaf.

Linguistic and communicative differences as well as the so-

---

1. Informants gave imprecise information about high school graduation. Many did not graduate because of low grades, especially in English. Failure to graduate is looked back on with shame, and consequently, some individuals made conflicting statements about graduation.

cialization process have functioned to separate deaf people from the rest of society. These factors have resulted in the formation of a community of deaf people. As will be seen, the formation of this community begins in childhood.

THE DEAF COMMUNITY

Anthropologists have been particularly concerned with the analysis of small communities. The concept of the "little community" is of a group of people bound together, not only by geographic ties but by smallness, homogeneity, group consciousness, and self-sufficiency (Redfield, 1955:4). This concept has become practically synonymous with simple, preindustrial society. Within the United States, however, such groups can still be found—for example, certain American Indian tribes (Lee, 1959) and religious sects such as the Hutterites (Eaton, 1952). These groups are bound together by shared symbolic systems, such as language, as well as by a repertoire of shared customs and values that differ from the mainstream of society. Such a group is the deaf community.

Whether the deaf community is really a community has been widely debated. The deaf population of the United States, however, does define itself as a community (Jacobs, 1974). Members of the deaf community themselves have suggested that the word *subculture* indicates a significant degree of separateness from society and implies major value orientations that are at odds with society. The word *community*, which they prefer, suggests that a person is still part of his or her culture without the separation inferred in the word *subculture*. The deaf community has been defined in a variety of ways. Most writers on the subject agree that the shared social world is the key to the deaf community (Schein, 1968). Actual definitions of the deaf community, however, are generally based on other criteria.

Definitions that arise from audiologic causes infer that membership in the group is based on hearing loss that prevents the individual from having sustained interaction with his or her environment. In defining this group Schein (1968) includes those persons who have severely limited audiologic capabilities, as well as a smaller number of people who have a hearing loss that does not necessarily preclude audition in the speech frequencies. These latter individuals are "socially deaf."

Another perspective is that of the deaf community as an ethnic or minority group (Vernon and Makowsky, 1969; Padden and Markowicz, 1975), a concept based on Barth's (1969: 13–14) definition of ethnic memberships as ascriptive and related to one's identity. If a person identifies with a group and is identified by others as a member of that group, the person is then perceived as a group member, sharing characteristics which the group holds in common—language, lifestyle, and values (Barth, 1969). There is a strong sense of group identification in the deaf community, based on shared experiences of the disability.

The deaf community has also been defined on the basis of the common linguistic bond—the knowledge of American Sign Language (Schlesinger and Meadow, 1972; Newman, 1974).

AMERICAN SIGN LANGUAGE

Since Whorf (1956) first theorized the connection between language, cognition, and social reality anthropologists have given increased attention to these relationships in the study of culture. The main purpose of language is to communicate with one's fellow human beings. Each language has its own idiosyncrasies that influence social relationships (Frake, 1964). Language has played a crucial role in the development of the deaf community. As a result, the deaf community can be defined as a linguistic community (Gumperz, 1962: 31).

American Sign Language is the first language of most deaf Americans. It is distinct from English, and follows a different grammatical and syntactical construction (Stokoe, 1960). Finger-spelling is used interchangeably with sign language and consists of a symbol for each letter of the alphabet. By putting together these symbols in different ways, a person can spell on the fingers anything that can be expressed in English, from the simple to the complex.

American Sign Language is based on a sign language system brought to the United States from France 150 years ago (Meadow, 1972:20). Sign language systems based on English syntax have been introduced in the past few years. Prior to that, however, American Sign Language was the only system of manual signs in common use among deaf people in the United States, and today it is the main means of communication for most deaf adults.

Sign language has long been taboo in schools, which stress the teaching of lip-reading and speech production. In the past, stigma was attached to the use of sign language, and vestiges of this stigma persist. The ongoing controversy over sign language and the continual efforts by deaf people to maintain it in the schools (often without success) has resulted in American Sign Language becoming a threatened language.

There is considerable concern among deaf people that American Sign Language, which is used to fulfill the communication needs of daily life, be preserved unchanged. American Sign Language, which is used expressively, is a symbolic badge of identity in the deaf community.

A knowledge of English is an important part of life in American culture. Despite the effort to learn English, reading and writing remain a problem for most deaf adults. It is difficult to get a conceptual grasp of the language without having heard it.

The need to communicate in both American Sign Language and written English requires double linguistic mastery, something most deaf people do not have. Most deaf people read and write at a fifth-grade level or below (Furth, 1966:205). They are confused by words with dual meanings, by the addition of new words to the language, and by colloquial expressions. The linguistic and communicative differences that occur as a result of early childhood deafness further separate the deaf from society and help to create the deaf community.

The Emergence of Community

The lives of the deaf, like those of other old people, are influenced by events that occurred in the past, as well as by their present life. Early childhood experiences that revolve around deafness shape the course of the deaf person's life and profoundly affect the aging process. This chapter describes the early life of members of the study population: how these people became deaf, how their families reacted to the deafness, how they began their first forays into the worlds of the hearing and became acquainted with the other deaf, and how these encounters shaped their perception of themselves as occupying a "marginal" status.

LANGUAGE ACQUISITION AND THE SOCIALIZATION PROCESS

The detection of disability in a child results in the parents experiencing guilt, denial, self-doubt, and chronic sorrow (Davis, 1963). Informants report that their parents were distressed and didn't know how to deal with the deafness.

The emotional difficulties that parents experienced were exacerbated by the conflict over how to educate the child. These problems, combined with the inability of parent and child to communicate verbally, eventually weakened the parent-child bond.

Mrs. Moore's first memory is of the conflict that arose in her family because of her deafness. When she was two and a half years old, [1] *Mrs. Moore (now eighty years old) and two of her nine siblings were infected with spinal meningitis, which was epidemic at the turn of the century.* [2] *Her sister died, but Mrs. Moore and her brother survived with no apparent residual disability.* [3] *As she grew her parents noticed that she had stopped talking and babbling. "As children grow they start to talk. Not me. Quiet. Mother thought, 'What's wrong with her? Could she be deaf?'* [4] *So she went to see the minister."*

When Mrs. Moore's mother went to see the minister, he suggested that Mrs. Moore be sent to the California School for the Deaf. This suggestion embroiled the whole family in a debate that continued for a number of years. Her mother liked

1. Age at the time of hearing loss is an important factor in defining the population. The later the hearing loss is acquired, the more likely the child is to have acquired language prior to it. Hearing loss that occurs after acquisition of language is considered adventitious. If the deafness occurs before the age of two years, it is generally termed prelingual (Meadow, 1975); however, we can postulate that any hearing the child may have before the age of two will be of benefit in acquiring language. Two-thirds of the subsample reported they lost their hearing before their first birthday.
2. Infectious diseases and fevers accounted for the cause of deafness for over half the subjects in the subsample.
3. No one in the subsample had a second disability. In this regard they were characteristic of the group as a whole, none of whom had multiple handicaps.
4. Wherever the communicative style of the informant presents the underlying feeling of the quote more clearly, I have preserved it without translation.

the idea. Her father, however, thought it would heap stigma on the family and disgrace them.

Mrs. Moore dramatically enacted this family argument. She said, "My father did not want me to go to a deaf asylum. He thought the other farm families would think there was something wrong with our family—having a person locked away in an asylum." Her mother finally prevailed, reiterating that it was "school." Her mother packed and fought with her father while Mrs. Moore watched. Her father was yelling, "Institutions are for crazy people—my daughter is not crazy," and her mother responded with "No, she must go. She has to learn to read and write so she won't be stupid." Mrs. Moore did finally go away to school at five and a half years. Each summer, when she returned home from school, the argument between her parents would start anew, and she would anxiously await the fall, afraid that her father would prevent her from returning to school. The theme of emotional upheaval typifies the early life histories of the informants.

Most researchers who study early child development assume that the child is spontaneously learning the language of his or her culture, and that the parents' language is the means by which the child is socialized (Brown, 1962:285). In other words, language acquisition and socialization proceed together. Normal children learn their native tongue by hearing people speak it, from the time they are born, and acquire language between the ages of one and a half and three and a half years (McNeill, 1965:16).

The process of spontaneous language learning and socialization does not take place naturally in the deaf child, except among deaf children who have deaf parents (Meadow, 1968:30). Early childhood deafness is thus a unique exception to a process that occurs universally among normal children. Because culture is transmitted through language, the socialization process in deaf children is delayed until language is provided. For the sample the delay lasted until the child began his or her education at the age of five or six years.

Educational philosophies and techniques have had a profound influence on group formation among the aged deaf and have created boundaries within the deaf community akin to ethnic boundaries. The result of this controversy in social terms has been to divide the deaf population into oralists and signers, who sometimes cannot communicate with each other except through writing.

The oral method means that the person communicates by lip-reading and speech production. The ambiguity of lip-reading and speech production causes considerable frustration for the individual who cannot hear speech (see the Glossary). Most informants who were taught this method reported their inability to rely only on lip-reading and speech production for communication.

The manual (signing) method incorporates a system of specific signs for given words with finger-spelling, so that all information is communicated by the hands. The manual method is now practically extinct in institutional teaching, having given way to a method called total communication that focuses on both sign language and speech production and reception.

The controversy over oral versus signing methods of education has raged among educators of the deaf for over a hundred years. Feelings run high among deaf people, their relatives, and educators of the deaf. The "victim" of the controversy is the deaf individual, who often complains bitterly of its effect on him or her. Mr. Chase echoed many of his peers when he said, "That's what made me dumb, that oral training. It did me no good."

The ultimate choice that parents made about the method of education to be used was influenced by a number of factors, especially knowledge of available alternatives. The options varied from one state and locality to the next. In the San Francisco Bay Area sixty years ago there were three major educational routes for the deaf child: (1) the State School for the Deaf at Berkeley, where children boarded and learned sign language; (2) St. Joseph's School for the Deaf, a parochial boarding school that taught primarily in the oral method; and (3) various schools in San Francisco and Oakland that taught day students the oral method.

Family communication patterns were established at the time the child's first school was chosen, if not before. Mrs. Hanley had a great-aunt who was deaf, so when her parents realized she was deaf too, they began to use the gesture system of idiosyncratic "home signs" they had used with the aunt. They communicated with her in this way until they sent her to school at the age of ten. Fifty or sixty years ago, the parent who learned sign language was a rarity. Most children with hearing parents had no meaningful communication at home.

This barrier to communication has had a variety of results among the individuals I studied. Siblings often learned some sign language and became go-betweens or interpreters for their deaf brother or sister and their parents. Most frequently the deaf child who learned to communicate in sign language, however, could not communicate with most family members except through writing. The long-term effects of the communication barrier affected the child's relationships with the family of origin long after he or she grew up.

SOCIALIZATION AT HOME

Children who attended oral schools tended to live at home with their families. All of the people in the sample who went to oral schools had parents with normal hearing. Parents took on the primary socialization responsibilities for their children, using oral techniques such as careful enunciation to communicate with their child; however, these efforts were not always successful. The difficulties of using the oral method with pre-lingually deaf children are dramatically outlined by Spradley and Spradley (1978).

The dinner table, the symbol of family togetherness and primary forum for the socialization of children among middle-class families in the United States, has become a symbol of isolation and even alienation for many deaf individuals. Informants used inclusion or exclusion at the dinner table as their index of participation in family life. Mr. Creasy said, "They always ignored me at the dinner table, so when I was old enough I left home and started my own family."

While the socialization process was fraught with communication difficulties for many people, those who could communicate with their parents perceived it positively. Successful oralists look back on the socialization process as a measure of their parents' love and devotion, and their ties with their parents remained strong. One informant said, "My mother taught me everything I know. She really prepared me to deal with life."

The degree to which identity influences present modes of communication among these individuals varies from one person to the next. Regardless of the way in which people communicate in adulthood, most individuals who began their school career in an oral school think of themselves as oralists. Their identification with the mode is second only to gender identity and deaf identity.[5]

Children who were enrolled in oral schools had to hide any knowledge of sign language from their parents and other adults. This presented a major problem to many people, as it intimated a secret life of which their parents disapproved, a feeling which has persisted into old age. Mrs. Grainger, who

5. Most people with oral educations are able to communicate in sign language, and in adulthood they use sign language in socializing and at home.

learned sign language at the age of five and was then sent to an oral school, said, "I never used sign language at home. My mother didn't approve of it. She worked hard to give me a good oral education." Some people accepted this dichotomy —speaking and lip-reading with their parents at home and signing with their friends away from home—while others resented it. Mr. Bradshaw said, "I love my family. But I would love them more if they had accepted sign language."

The identity struggle of the deaf individual who was exposed to both methods is typified by Miss Sarah Ainsley, a sixty-four-year-old retired counselor. Typical, too, are the decisions made by her family that created a classic double-bind situation and facilitated the internalization of conflict.

Miss Ainsley was born in Seattle, where her father was a teacher. She is the third of four children. The other three children have normal hearing. When she was pregnant with her, Miss Ainsley's mother was ill with rubella. Miss Ainsley attributes her deafness to this illness. Although she appeared to be normal when she was born, she seldom responded to people. Her parents thought she was mentally retarded until she was two years old. At that time her grandmother came to visit and diagnosed her deafness by yelling at her from behind a door.

After her deafness was diagnosed, her parents took her to many doctors, looking for a cure. One physician forced both of his fists into Miss Ainsley's mouth in an effort to open up blocked passages. After much expense Miss Ainsley's parents finally gave up their hope of finding a cure for her deafness. She looks back on these efforts as a set of painful, humiliating experiences.

Miss Ainsley began her education at an oral day school when she was five years old. Shortly thereafter her parents heard that another family was offering private tutoring to a deaf child the same age as their daughter. The other family wanted to give their child peer contact. Miss Ainsley was accepted for this special tutoring. She spent the next three years of her life in private lessons that focused primarily on speech development and lip-reading. Of this experience she says, "I was real proud of myself. Here I was, a little deaf kid—I traveled all the way there and home by myself."

When Miss Ainsley was eight years old, the family moved to a Southern state where her father had been offered a job. The only school for deaf children was the state institution, where sign language was used. Miss Ainsley spent the next ten years of her life there. In retrospect she says, "It was a real shock to me. I went around for about a month in a state of fear and anxiety."

She learned sign language by watching people who spoke and signed at the same time. She lip-read them to get the meaning of each sign. She learned finger-spelling by looking it up in the dictionary and teaching it to herself. Miss Ainsley thought of herself as different from the other children. Not only did she communicate differently, but her family had passed their high academic standards on to her. According to Miss Ainsley, the institution had very low standards of academic achievement and expectations. She said, "The other children all came from farms."

Her parents maintained a negative attitude toward sign language, even though they had placed her in a signing school. She said, "My mother was a social climber—she is still that way." Her mother did not want her to be around deaf people who used sign language, because of its stigma. Every summer she would get lonely at home and prepare to bicycle to a friend's house. Her mother would see her getting ready to go

*out, and she would say, "Where are you going? Oh, please
don't go there—I don't like to see you with those deaf."
    When she graduated she got a job in another state. "When I
left home after graduation, I stopped paying attention to my
parents' ideas about whom I should associate with and how I
should communicate."*

Miss Ainsley was caught between the realities of her education and the desires of her parents. It was impossible to reconcile this conflict. Miss Ainsley has spent the rest of her life trying to placate her family. Knowledgeable and occupationally
successful, she is unsure of herself in interpersonal relationships. She has never married and maintains a marked aloof-
ness from others. She has no close friends.

Miss Ainsley is articulate when she discusses the controversy in which she has been embroiled all her life and the
stigma of deafness. She is unable to resolve her inner conflict,
whether to be a member of the deaf community or a member of
the hearing world. Each time she communicates with others
the conflict arises, to be dealt with again and again. The inner
conflict experienced by Miss Ainsley continues during the entire life-span of others with similar early life experiences.

The goal of an oral education is the preparation of a deaf
person to function as a "normal" person with hearing friends
and a broad range of interests. Such a feat is a rarity. Oralists in
the sample interact socially with people with normal hearing
in a very restricted way or not at all.

While the process of socialization and education differed
greatly in oral and manual circles, the same basic patterns developed in social relationships. Friendships with other deaf
people are based on early childhood association and mutual
experiences in the acquisition of language. These ties appear
to be equally strong among oralists and manualists. For this
reason, we can assume that the shared mutual experiences

resulting from the deafness itself are the basis of these enduring relationships, regardless of the way in which they were experienced.

THE SCHOOL AS PRIMARY SOCIALIZER

The role of the family in socializing the child was considerably diminished for those deaf children of hearing parents who boarded at school. As a result, the socialization and education processes occurred together, a unique situation in complex societies (Cohen, 1971). In the following section I shall discuss the effect of institutional socialization, which reflects the experiences of the majority of the group.

In the United States, institutionalization is generally seen as the last resort, whether it be commitment to a mental hospital, a nursing home for the aged, or an orphanage. Indeed, institutionalization is a stigmatizing experience for any child or adult, with its implicit assumption of rejection by one's family and by society. At the same time, it is a value of American society that children should be reared within the family, preferably by two parents. The family is seen as the optimum environment for the normal development of children, in contrast to the value placed by the Israelis on communal education (Spiro, 1965). When early childhood development takes place within an institution in the United States, the child is perceived as lacking the benefits that nurturing by the family provides and, consequently, as both vulnerable and incomplete in the eyes of society (Yarrow, 1964).

In order to teach deaf children systematically, state schools for the deaf were established in most states in the nineteenth century.[6] Mrs. Moore describes what life in the institution was like.

6. A few states with especially small populations had no residential schools at the turn of the century. These states sent deaf children to neighboring states to school. For example, children in Nevada were sent to California for their education.

"I learned everything I know at the Berkeley School. They taught me to sew and it saved my life!" When she went back to the farm each summer she darned all her brothers' work clothes. They paid her for doing this, and she, in turn, felt that through sewing she became a worthwhile member of her family.

When Mrs. Moore first arrived at the School, a deaf teacher taught her sign language, followed by reading and writing. She also had a class in lip-reading and speech, which helped to pacify her father. She learned to cook, as well as to sew, and she even learned how to iron there.

About her school years she says, "I liked learning, but the other girls made me unhappy. They called me 'the owl.' They said I was always watching, was too quiet, never talked. The teachers let them tease me. So I kept to myself."

Mrs. Moore was nine years old when the San Francisco earthquake and fire of 1906 occurred. She was in bed in the middle of the dormitory when everything started to shake and fall. The dormitory counselor ran in and signed that it was an earthquake; the students formed a line and marched to the basement. No one was hurt. A few weeks later someone came to get her in class, saying that her father had arrived at the school. "I was so surprised. He had come in person to make sure that his deaf daughter was all right!"

Going away to school also had its dark side. The emotional impact of the separation of the child from his or her family was profound. The individual child often saw it as a form of abandonment; parents were unable to impart their own philosophy of life to their child, and in giving the responsibility for rearing their child to the school, parents relinquished some of their investment in the child's development, thus diminishing the bonding that had taken place.

After they adjusted to the institution, however, children felt comfortable there. Many children did not want to go home in the summer, where communication was a problem. As Mr. Bauer reminded Mrs. Gray, "You used to cry all the way home on the train every summer." On the other hand, children who had deaf siblings accepted alternating periods of life at home and at school more philosophically. The separation from one's family, coupled with the emotional intensity surrounding the acquisition of language, was the basis for the development of a strong sense of group identification.

In the group of older deaf people I studied, the combination of parental rejection, institutionalization, and stigmatized language created an aura of social marginality that could not be dispelled. The individual who underwent this experience continues to be aware of the differences that set him or her apart from society.

Selma Haller, a retired milliner, has experienced the discontinuities that the majority of the sample expressed about being deaf. As one of three deaf children of hearing parents, she has had more opportunities than most deaf people to develop esteem-giving relationships within the family.

Mrs. Haller was born on a farm in Minnesota seventy-five years ago. Her parents emigrated from Finland, met, and married in Minnesota. Mrs. Haller is the youngest of five children, three of whom were born deaf.[7] When Mrs. Haller's mother was pregnant with her, her father died.

At about the time of Mrs. Haller's birth, her mother went shopping in a nearby town with Mrs. Haller's deaf brother. A couple of deaf peddlers saw the woman and her little boy gesturing to each other and wrote her a note telling her about the

---

7. When each parent has a recessive gene for deafness, it is likely that approximately half of their children will be deaf. There were 11 cases of congenital deafness among the subsample of 60.

state school for the deaf. The school was two hours away from home by train, and all three deaf children were eventually sent to this school, returning home only at Christmastime and in the summer.

Mrs. Haller's sister, Ellen, was born deaf two years before she was. These two formed a close bond, which has endured through the years. Her earliest memories are of following her sister around the yard. She says, "I was her 'step'n-fetch-it.' I always thought she was wonderful." They played together constantly.

By the time she was born, her brother and her mother had learned some signs, so that she grew up with a means of expressing herself. When she was five and Ellen was seven, they were sent together to the school for the deaf. When her brother had first gone there, the school had used the oral method. By the time Mrs. Haller began school, however, the school was using the manual method. According to Mrs. Haller, her brother never did become proficient in sign language. In contrast, Mrs. Haller developed an excellent command of American Sign Language as well as some proficiency in written English.

Mrs. Haller experienced no distress about attending the state school because her brother had already been sent there. She enjoyed school and she also enjoyed going home for the summer. She graduated from the state school when she was eighteen years old.

Mrs. Haller was fortunate to be the last child born in her family. The gradual acceptance of deafness in her family has helped her to adjust to her disability. She went to school preceded and accompanied by older siblings. In addition, she received a consistent education, which enabled her to develop good communication skills. Nevertheless, Mrs. Haller is still trying to resolve her disability in adulthood. She is well aware of the discontinuities between the hearing and the deaf world. Most deaf people continue to experience considerable ambivalence about themselves and their disability. The ways in which people deal with these identity issues will be discussed in chapter four.

The institutional experience had a different effect and meaning for deaf children of deaf parents. As was mentioned earlier, deaf children of deaf parents acquire language at the same time as do normal children. Those few individuals in the sample who had deaf parents were the only ones who did not experience delayed socialization. Whether the child of such a family went to the state school as a day student or as a boarding student, the transition was considered a natural one by both parents and child. Parents felt that the school would continue to instill values and a linguistic mode which they espoused for their children. For this reason, going to school was seen as a natural step toward the child's future leadership role in the community.

The difference in self-perception between those descended from generations of deaf people and those descended from hearing people is marked. Deaf people from deaf families can be characterized by a sense of complacency. This quality was present in every deaf person with deaf parents whom I interviewed, and was conspicuous by its absence from the rest of the sample.

Mr. John Bowker was born in New York City, the second of two deaf children born to deaf parents.[8] *When he was four years old the family moved to Buffalo so that the children could attend the Buffalo School for the Deaf, their parents' alma mater. His older sister and then he became day students*

8. As with all other deaf children of deaf parents, he began his own life history by telling me the history of his parents.

at the school, walking the short distance to school every day. He did well in school, as everyone had expected.

When he was fifteen he moved out of his parents' house and moved into the school dormitories so that he would have more time to socialize with his friends. Both he and his older sister followed this pattern, which their parents had anticipated. Mr. Bowker graduated from high school when he was eighteen years old. He had planned to go to Gallaudet College, but was prevented from doing so by the financial difficulties experienced by his family because of the Depression. Instead, he moved to San Francisco.

At sixty-eight Mr. Bowker, a retired glazier, is a leader in the deaf community. He takes his leadership role as a matter of course and seldom expresses doubts about his abilities. He considers himself a shrewd judge of character, although he is not especially introspective. He is deliberate, self-possessed, and in control of every situation, save those where hearing people are concerned. He admits that interaction with hearing people can be "ego-deflating," but this does not prevent him from interacting with them.

His one great disappointment in life was failure to go to Gallaudet College, thus missing out on the opportunity to become a leader of the deaf community on the national level. This disappointment is not related to any personal sense of failure, however. He takes his place in the community for granted. Mr. Bowker is comfortable with himself and with his social world.

The relationship between cultural continuity and identity development among the deaf is apparent. Both the continuity of language and the transmission of culture among deaf people descended from deaf parents produces a sense of self-acceptance. Beliefs and values are validated by the sense of cultural continuity in one's personal history. Deaf people with deaf forebears perceive themselves as part of a unique cultural tradition. They seek each other out because of the commonality of their experience. They seldom feel ambivalence or conflict about deafness, because the deaf community embodies their cultural tradition from the start.

The basic aim of the residential school, to socialize the child to live in the outside world, falls far short of its goal. When deaf children do leave the school, they are plagued by a series of misunderstandings and conflicts with people in the outside world. These problems result from the lack of opportunity to learn behavior appropriate to different life situations. Mrs. Jensen related how she and some other deaf adolescents tried to start a deaf club after graduation from the state school.

They needed a place to meet, but they did not know how to find one. A hearing person they knew suggested they contact the Chamber of Commerce. They did, and a few weeks later the Chamber of Commerce responded with a letter saying the young deaf people could have some space at the YMCA. Mrs. Jensen and her friends told everyone about it, and on the chosen date they all showed up. Mrs. Jensen said, "It was just awful. The room was in use. We had never responded to the Chamber of Commerce letter, letting them know we still wanted the space. So they gave it to someone else. And then we were too embarrassed to ask for another place. So we had to forget about starting a club. It was a great disappointment to me. But we were ignorant then, we didn't know any better."

The deaf child in a residential school has two social worlds: the world of teachers and parents and the world of other children. The nature of institutional life emphasizes the peer group, which becomes a surrogate family. In this respect, the deaf child's experience is similar to that of an age-graded peer group, such as the Xhosa (Mayer and Mayer, 1970), where socialization occurs primarily through peers. The strong bonds that are developed early in life are maintained into old age. The role of age-mates is central to the aged deaf individual's adaptive functioning and will be discussed in chapter six.

Deaf teachers, counselors, and hearing teachers who are the children of deaf persons pass on their own view of culture to the children, a perspective that differs somewhat from that of society in general. They emphasize the importance of participation in the deaf community and reinforce deaf identity. In the process of socialization, however, the goal of preparing children to learn behavior appropriate to the hearing world is often overlooked. When the individual leaves school, he or she is usually proficient in deaf social behavior and "ignorant" of the ways of the outside world.

Integration into society is difficult for any individual who has been removed to a closed environment that teaches about the outside world without offering experience of it directly. The institution itself develops its own culture (Goffman, 1961), which invariably differs in some ways from the rest of society. The child is thus both nurtured and given an identity within the institution, while the perceptual focus is on the social group. As Schlesinger (1972:22) points out, these children are expected to make the transition from communal living in the institution to the outside world, where the emphasis is on individualism.

Deaf children of hearing parents must discover for themselves workable variations of core American values, such as intense competitiveness, individualism, and social mobility, in order to survive as social beings. As a result of the need for face-to-face interaction, deaf people develop a high degree of social interdependence, which modifies core values. In the course of becoming adults they must resolve their value conflicts.

The residential school has a strong influence on the individual. In cultural terms, the group becomes a major part of the individual's perception because of its significance as a surrogate family. The focus on the group is part of a variant view of culture that is presented to deaf children in institutions and continually reinforced. Thus it becomes part of the socialization process. Like that of the Hopi (Lee, 1959), the world view of deaf people is of people in groups rather than as individuals. Therefore, the group becomes an organizing element in the social world of deafness. An orientation toward the group, which is taken for granted early in life, continues throughout the life cycle. This lifelong focus on the group rather than on the individual is in direct conflict with those American core values that emphasize individualism as good and collectivity as bad. In adult life this orientation both poses difficulties and offers advantages. As we shall see in later chapters, the group orientation is extremely adaptive in old age.

IV

Deafness:
Crucible of Identity

In chapter three I discussed how important the early life experiences are in community formation among the deaf. These experiences are also important in crystallizing identity, which in turn so strongly influences lifelong adaptation. In this chapter I shall discuss deaf identity and its implications for the development of specific coping mechanisms.

IDENTITY

Identity is a rudder that helps one steer through the cultural universe. It not only provides the individual with a sense of self, but enables him or her to relate that sense of self to the surrounding world. Our interaction with others is continuously affected by our identity. We must therefore be conscious of its social and cultural components. Clark and Kiefer (1971:6) define identity as "that cognitive structure which gives a sense of coherence, continuity, and social relatedness to one's image of oneself."

When I attended a political rally for older Californians with a group of deaf people, I observed a man dressed up as Uncle

Sam carrying a sign that said, "Senior Power." I turned to the people I was with and asked if they had considered using signs. They responded unanimously that if they did use them their signs would say "Deaf Power" rather than any other kind of power.

All the deaf people I spoke with during my research defined themselves primarily in terms of deafness; this identity is second only to gender. Deafness plays such a pivotal role in the self-concept of deaf people that at times it completely obscures the fact that the person has other attributes. Other aspects of identity are thus reduced to a fraction of the importance they might otherwise have for the individual. For example, ethnicity is usually an important part of a deaf person's identity. Nevertheless, most of the time it takes second place in relation to deaf identity.

Deaf identity is forged early in life and develops throughout the life-span. Mr. Shiller was eight years old when his deafness became a crucial and negative part of his self-image. His mother sent him from New York to San Francisco on the train by himself. When she said goodbye to him at the station, she hung on his chest a large sign that read "DEAF," so that the train conductors would look after him. "I was afraid she would find out if I took it off, so I left it on. You can imagine how people stared at me."

As the individual ages deafness defines the individual's relationship to society. For example, during World War II deaf people were not accepted for active military service (nor are they today). Although proud of their participation in the nation's war industry, the inability to fight symbolized their place in society once and for all and "clinched" their deaf identity.

By old age individual identity processes have undergone significant changes. Nevertheless, the day-to-day realities of being deaf continue to affect one's identity. Throughout life the deaf person is in a continual identity conflict, made explicit in interactions with hearing people because these interactions call attention to the deaf person's inadequacies.

While on a trip to Reno Mrs. Gray decided to play Keno. Half an hour later she returned to a group of her deaf friends, looking shaken. "I'm so mortified," she said; "the dealer gave me some instructions, and I guess I didn't understand them, because I did something wrong and she bawled me out. I couldn't get out of there fast enough."

Interaction with other deaf people, on the other hand, tends to reinforce positive feelings about one's abilities and validates one's worth as an individual. Regardless of the actual quantity of interaction with either hearing or deaf people, however, the symbolic conflict is kept alive in the person's mind by the inconsistencies between self-perception in the in-group and the way one is perceived in dealing with the outside world.

Symbols of stigma are the ever-present reminders of what Goffman (1963) calls spoiled identity. Sign language is the visible indicator of stigma for the deaf individual.

Tellingly, sign language has a large number of signs for inferior mental ability, such as stupid, ignorant, pea-brain, know-nothing, and dummy. The linguistic elaboration is an indication of the perception of inferiority that is built into the culture. One informant demonstrated how he felt about himself when he said to me, "I'm dumb. . . . You're hearing—smart," and another informant said of herself, "Me—no voice —dumb." This perception, which correlates hearing with intelligence and deafness with dumbness, was almost universal in individuals' comments.

Hearing-deaf interactions are characterized by ambiguity. Ambiguity regarding the degree of impairment in disability has the most negative effect on interpersonal relationships (Zahn, 1973:116). As one informant commented, "People often talk to me and I can't answer. I shake my head and point to my ear. But they don't understand—they think I'm stuck up." These comments reflect the importance of social perception and its influence on self-image (George Herbert Mead, 1934).

Many of the individuals in the sample state that they came to terms with problems of self-worth as they aged. Wallace (1967: 71) calls this process "identity work." When resolution of identity conflict does occur, it is usually stated very simply. As one informant said, "I have learned to like myself."

Others like themselves, but with reservations. They would rather be hearing. Mrs. Gray said, "I'm sure people have said to you, 'I'm happy I'm deaf.' Well, I have never wanted to be deaf. What's so good about it? I would much rather be able to hear and speak clearly, like you do." Mrs. Gray is extremely realistic about her deafness. It is her way of coping with her disability. In contrast, most deaf people have a need to find something of value about their disability, to justify it to themselves and turn it into something with positive qualities. They continually try to find strength in themselves and in their social world through the development of various styles of coping. The following cases depict different ways in which people strain to create a positive self-image, a process that continues into old age.

AMBIVALENCE

Mrs. Haller, whose childhood experience was discussed in chapter three, has spent her life wrestling with the question of whether it is better to be hearing or deaf. A tall, stately woman of seventy-five, Mrs. Haller has an engaging friendly manner and seems to be at her ease with both deaf and hearing people.

As a child, Mrs. Haller came home from the state school every summer. One summer when she was a teenager she had an experience that profoundly colored her view of herself. The family lived in a small town and owned a farm on its outskirts. She volunteered to go collect eggs at the farm. Some time after she left, her brother realized that the train would be coming through and that Mrs. Haller always walked on the tracks. So he started to run after her. When he finally caught up with Mrs. Haller, the brother pointed back in the direction from which they had both come and they could see the train off in the distance.

Mrs. Haller says of this experience, "It changed the way I think of myself. It made me feel very vulnerable and different from everyone else. I don't think I realized what it meant to be deaf before that happened. I stopped being happy-go-lucky and became cautious when I went anywhere. I am still that way—very careful, and alert."

Mrs. Haller's changing self-perception was further influenced by the dilemma she faced when she began to date. She was attracted to hearing men and received proposals of marriage from four such men. She ultimately declined each proposal because she felt that a hearing-deaf marriage would have too many problems. "It's hard to maintain a good social life when your husband is hearing."

Mrs. Haller eventually married a deaf man. She describes her husband: "He could speak—he was just like a hearing person but was stone deaf." He lost his hearing when he was seven years old. "He knew a lot; he knew how to act [with people]." He wanted to be an engineer, so when he was eighteen he went to Washington, D.C., and attended Gallaudet College and another college at the same time. "At the hearing college he passed for hearing—he lip-read everyone. Then one day while he was at the hearing college he ran into one of his Gallaudet professors, who said, 'You can't go to school *here. You're deaf,' and he had my husband dismissed from school. My husband was so discouraged he gave it all up and came home."*

This misfortune deeply affected the way Mr. Haller viewed the world. He became wary of the hearing world and passed this attitude on to his wife.

Now a widow, Mrs. Haller says, "I still miss my husband. He taught me about the hearing world." She leads an active social life in the deaf community. She has many close friends, primarily other women, and spends most of her time visiting them and being visited, playing cards, and talking. She has constructed her social world so that social contact with hearing people is her option. In fact, curiosity about the hearing world brings her into frequent social contact with hearing people, usually with those who approach the deaf community in order to learn about deafness or sign language.

In old age Mrs. Haller continues her lifelong thirst for knowledge of the hearing world. She goes to many of the educational and informational activities held for deaf people, such as museum tours in sign language. She writes letters in support of more signed and captioned programs on television. And she asks questions, such as "I saw a word in the newspaper the other day, schizophrenic. What does that mean?"

In old age Mrs. Haller is a popular, energetic woman who has considerable status among her peers. Nevertheless, she is always trying to reconcile her place in a hearing world. She questions, compares, and reassures herself about the behavior of deaf and hearing people. For example, she says, "My son tells me some deaf make funny noises when they eat or talk. I hope I don't do that, do I?" She rethinks old issues, such as "Is it better to marry another deaf person if you are deaf yourself?" In her own relationships she has aligned herself with several people who are "like" hearing people—for example, her "speaking" husband, and two "speaking" women friends.[1] She also has several deaf friends who are married to hearing men.

It is in her analysis of the behavior of others that her ambivalence about deafness comes out. An example is a story about a married couple who are her acquaintances. According to Mrs. Haller, the husband, a hearing man, was a sailor when he met his wife for the first time. He whistled at a girl, and when she did not respond, he followed her. When he found out she was deaf, he was fascinated. They started to date and eventually married. Mrs. Haller commented, "Funny how deafness makes a difference." Mrs. Haller's innuendo in this story is that deaf women are more appealing to men than are hearing women.

Mrs. Haller is critical of behavior she has observed among hearing people that she considers callous and inconsiderate. Her criticism is triggered by the rejection she senses from hearing people. She tells the story of a woman who lost her hearing when she was a teenager, whereupon all of her hearing friends "dropped her." "Funny," says Mrs. Haller; "why are hearing [people] like that?" Mrs. Haller fights off the threat of her own potential rejection by being exclusive herself.

Mrs. Haller is never completely comfortable about her own relationship to the world. One way in which she deals with this discomfort is by talking about herself. She is continually reconstructing her biography, reexamining the details of her life. This process is stimulated by the discontinuities in the environment (Kiefer, 1974:232). Mrs. Haller is typical of many people in the sample who continually reconstruct their biographies. The underlying purpose of this behavior is to give a sense of consistency to events and actions that take place over the life course. At the same time, resolution of old identity conflicts may take place.

---

1. Such individuals either have a moderate hearing loss or lost their hearing after the age of three, hence their speech is intelligible.

ANGER

Some deaf people never resolve their identity problems at all and continue to express anger and frustration at a hearing world with which they feel at odds. This sense of frustration was expressed in a story told by Mr. Jack Taylor, a seventy-year-old married man. He said, "I heard there used to be a deaf man locked up on Alcatraz [a former federal prison]. They shouldn't have done that—cruel to the poor deaf. They say his name sign was 'Lonely.'" This story evokes the sense of isolation experienced by all deaf people. The prison in the story symbolizes the way walls are erected by society to sentence them to isolation. In particular, this story symbolizes the way Mr. Taylor views his own life. As he relates the story of his life, his feelings of anger and injustice are very evident.

Mr. Taylor is the only deaf person in his family of orientation. When he was five years old, his parents sent him to the state school for two years. Then, when he was seven, his parents sent him to an oral school, and he stayed there until he was high school age, when he was sent back to the state school. His parents emphasized the importance of developing good speech, and he failed to live up to their expectations. His parents never understood his speech, so he had to rely on his brother to interpret for him. He said that later on in his own family his son always used to criticize his speech. "Now, at last there are no hearing living with me to tell me what they think of my speech."

Mr. Taylor has had one job in his life, as a "jack of all trades" for a machinery company. When I asked him if he repaired the machines, he said, "No, [I'm] deaf, but I always knew what was wrong with them," indicating that his deafness prevented him from becoming a machinist, a more prestigious job. Mr. Taylor worked for the company for almost fifty years, starting soon after he finished high school. He said, "Deaf people have always had trouble getting jobs, so I never tried to find anything else."

Now retired, Mr. Taylor participates in the activities of several deaf senior citizen groups. He was recently invested with considerable responsibility for one organization. Much of his time is spent in the affairs of this group. He has little contact with hearing people in old age and prefers it this way. He says, with a disparaging wave of the hand, "Hearing people—talk, talk, talk. I can't understand them. They should learn sign language."

Despite this attitude, in public encounters Mr. Taylor still tries to pass as a hearing person. Recently he learned that the checker in the grocery store he has shopped at for twenty years is herself hard of hearing and knows sign language. As he related this story, he looked rueful, and his wife burst into laughter. "Can you beat that? All these years Jack has been worrying about keeping up appearances, and the joke's on him."

The limitations with which the deaf individual must work, such as limited communication ability, lack of jobs with opportunity for advancement, and limited access to mass media, necessitates an adjustment in the individual's value orientation. Instead of internalizing the variations in values in the deaf community which put emphasis on sociability rather than on achievement, some individuals continue to apply the values of the general society to themselves. Individuals, like Mr. Taylor, who continue to cherish the values of the mainstream set themselves up to maximize frustration. Such a situation, in turn, prevents the individual from resolving identity problems.

Mr. Taylor is bitter about all of the troubles he has had. He is especially angry at some of the hearing people who are central figures in his life. He castigates his parents and his boss for their difficulty in communicating with him and for their impatience with him. He has only negative things to say about hearing people, and only positive things to say about deafness. He says, "Me, I'm happy to be deaf. All that noise—I don't have to listen to it. I would hate it."

Mr. Taylor's anger at the hearing world is shared to a degree by his peers. His complaints and stories are tolerated and ignored by his friends. They understand and sympathize with him, but they try to discourage him from overdoing it. The extent of his anger makes people uncomfortable and reminds them of their own interactions with hearing people that they would rather forget.

In old age, the sources of stress for Mr. Taylor—his boss, parents, and children—no longer have a daily impact on his life. This factor, coupled with the tolerance his peers exhibit, helps him cope more effectively in old age than he has in the past. Like Mr. Taylor, most deaf people experience a decrease in stressful interaction in old age, a factor that enhances their coping ability.

Most people never do completely resolve their ambivalence about their deafness. Communication problems in social interaction arise too frequently for resolution to take place. Negative feelings about deafness can be balanced by other esteem-giving factors, such as pride in one's accomplishments, or interactions which reflect positively on one's social identity.

PRIDE

Mr. Peter Ciano is a seventy-two-year-old married man. He was born in San Francisco shortly after his parents arrived in the United States from Italy. The language he was learning when he lost his hearing at the age of three years was Italian. He started school at the age of five, when he was sent to the Berkeley School for the Deaf.

Mr. Ciano, a carpenter by trade, thinks of himself as a family man. Shortly after he moved to Oakland as a young man, he met his wife-to-be at a deaf social, "a nice Italian girl," and they courted for several years before getting married. Mrs. Ciano worked in a laundry until they began to have children. Mr. Ciano looks back with fond memories on the time the family was together. We were sitting in his kitchen. He rubbed the table with his hand and said, "This was always the center of activity. The whole family would sit around in the kitchen every evening. Those were good times." He is extremely proud of the accomplishments of their three children. One is an English teacher and another is a teacher of the deaf.

Mr. and Mrs. Ciano divide their time between socializing with their family and with other deaf people. Mr. Ciano spends a lot of time fishing with both deaf and hearing cronies. He bowls with a senior citizen group of hearing people once a week. The Cianos spend most weekends with their children and grandchildren who live in the area.

Mr. Ciano is an informal leader of his age-mates and is well liked. His prestige is related to his former occupation as a carpenter, his role as a family man, and as a person long active in the deaf community. He is warm and outgoing and is friendly toward both hearing and deaf strangers who approach the group. He has a number of close friends, especially among the other Italian deaf.

Despite Mr. Ciano's deafness, for the most part he has been able to live his life according to the values and expectations of his family. His parents attached great importance to family life, and Mr. Ciano feels he has carried on this tradition. "I have my wife. I have two great-grandchildren. The family, the name, will continue. What more can I ask for?" His pride in his family compensates for the feelings of inferiority he expresses about his deafness.

Mr. Ciano has been less successful in carrying out the familial expectations about wealth and achievement. Deaf people are well aware of and generally unable to live up to the expectations of achievement of American society. Negative comparisons with their own families of origin mirror their comparisons between themselves and the rest of society. Mr. Ciano says, "We've always been poor—just enough to get by. It's ironic—my own family are all well off."

He has been successful in providing for his family, however. On my first visit to his home he wanted to make sure that I realized he was self-sufficient. He said to me, "I want you to know that, although we are deaf, we pay taxes. We own our own home." His wife said to him, "She knows that—it's not necessary to tell her that." He responded, "I just want her to know that I'm not some poor deaf. I worked for forty-five years. Not all deaf are helpless." Although proud of his accomplishments, Mr. Ciano is afraid that he will be stereotyped because of his disability and will be seen as dependent on society for support.

Mr. Ciano fights feelings of inferiority about deafness by emphasizing other aspects of life in which he takes pride. In public he appears to be jovial and self-assured. He seeks out both deaf and hearing people and goes to great lengths to overcome communication difficulties. He is respected for his ability to get along with hearing and deaf people alike. His role as a goodwill ambassador for his age-mates provides him with considerable self-esteem and reinforces positive aspects of social identity.

The deaf derive considerable satisfaction from doing the same basic things that people with normal hearing do: they marry, have children, work, buy property, retire. In old age, when people look back on their achievements, they gain a sense of well-being that stems from their own accomplishments and the knowledge that comes with experience.

that their children were hearing. Often these individuals expressed the greatest sense of inferiority related to their own deafness. Mrs. Riley said proudly, "There are no deaf in our family. All our children can hear." In some cases, the same people complained bitterly about the poor quality of their relationships with their children and grandchildren. Unresolved feelings about the disability are probably communicated to the children, thus heightening the stigma attached to the disability. Men did not relate this issue to their children except in general terms—for example, "I came from a deaf family and I liked the companionship," or "Funny that my kids are hearing and my brother's kids are deaf."

Most common among both men and women were comments about shared ethnicity or religion, such as "We were both Italian." Another kind of homogeneity that is important is homogeneity of communicative mode. Most oralists are married to other oralists, most manualists to other manualists. Some individuals in the sample who crossed this boundary to marry have worked it out to their mutual satisfaction, while others have not. It is a potential source of conflict.

THE DEAF FAMILY

The limited ties with extended kin reinforce the tendency of deaf people to form nuclear families. Deaf men and women begin the process of reconciling their disability in earnest when they start their own family. In the process of establishing one's own family, the deaf individual is creating an environment where deafness is the norm rather than the exception. The process of making a home, developing a relationship with a spouse, and rearing children creates the potential for personal growth and development that it holds for all people. But more than that, for the first time it allows the deaf individual to take responsibility for himself or herself, to develop autonomy; it gives the deaf person the opportunity to assume a cen-

V

Family Life

Although, as we have seen in chapter three, the peer group played a vital role in the early and middle childhood of people in this sample, the adult years for the deaf reintroduces the family as a principal arena of social life. In this chapter I shall discuss the important role that family life plays in the adaptive strategies that people develop as they age.

Deaf children who have had little contact with deaf adults frequently have no conception of what their life will be like in adulthood. They ask basic questions about themselves, such as "What will happen when I grow up? Will I become hearing?" Without role models, the deaf child may be unsure about many things, such as the place of marriage and children in the deaf person's life.

Of her own anticipation of adulthood Mrs. Moore said, "I taught my youngest brothers and sisters sign language when I came home from school in the summer time. That started me thinking—if I could teach them I could teach children of my own. That's when I realized deaf people could marry and have children." Familial relationships for the aged deaf are structured by American middle-class family forms as well as by communication barriers. Ties with one's spouse and children may be intensified because they are usually free of such barriers, whereas ties with siblings and grandchildren may be tenuous. The marital relationship may be invested with particular intensity because of its lack of communication barriers.

In the general American population, 9 persons out of 10 marry at some time in their lives (Streib, 1970:30). Within the subsample of 60 people, 5 people, or 8 percent, never married. All but one of the never-married people were teachers and counselors in state schools, jobs that provide individuals with quasi-familial roles. Of the remaining 55 people, all have been married: 42 once, 8 twice, and 5 three times.

Of 60 individuals in the subsample, 76 percent have been married once for a mean period of forty years. Of the 55 people in the subsample who married, 14 people, or one-fourth, have been divorced. Of these 14, 6 have been married to each other in the past, an indication of the bounded nature of the relationships in the deaf community.

The basic family unit in old age in the United States is the marital dyad. Fifty-three percent of people sixty-five years of age and older are married couples (Riley et al., 1968:159). At the time of this study, almost two-thirds, or 65 percent, of the subsample were married.

THE BASIS OF MARRIAGE

Mrs. Moore says of her husband, "I chose him because I knew he would be right for me, but our families were against the match. They said it was because I was a Protestant and he was Catholic, but I think it was also because both of us were deaf. We refused to stop seeing each other, though, and finally they gave in—to love."

Among deaf informants mate selection was based on a combination of romantic and practical ideas. Marriages are predominantly endogamous. People tend to marry other deaf people because of their shared experiences and shared expectations. Less conflict was anticipated by both sexes in marriage to another deaf person. One informant explained that he came

close to marrying a hearing woman, but that he hesi cause he was deaf. Only one person in the subsample married to a person with normal hearing.

Individuals related the limited supply of potential the deaf community to the need to find the right s] young adulthood and go through life with that perso men and women expressed the concern they had exp in their youth that appropriate partners would be sna[The number of potential mates in young adulthood ther decreased by relationships that were established hood and adolescence and that eventually culminatec riage.

Women were more pragmatic about marriage th were in all cases, perhaps because they had feelings o vulnerability because of their lack of job skills and [earning ability. Mrs. DiLucchia said, "It was hard t good husband. I wanted someone who was a steady v

Men tended to be romantic and vague. The pragn proach of women vis-à-vis men may be true of A women in general. Kirkpatrick and Hobart (1954) fou American men romanticize their mates more than do can women. Mr. Harrison said, "I saw her and I knew the one," while another informant said his impressic meeting his wife-to-be was that she was a "sweet girl." He married her two weeks later.

Women voiced their concerns about deafness in c while men did not express concern. Some women want deaf children. Mrs. Winters said, "Two men wer ing me in college. One was deaf. The other was hard-ing. I chose the hard-of-hearing man because I felt my of having hearing children were better." Others fel didn't matter. Mrs. Graves said, "I knew it was a possi didn't bother me at all [that one or more child might be

The question of prestige arises in relation to the a one's children to hear. Some women were proud of

tral role in family life. Becoming part of a family, and all that it entails, thus plays a crucial role in lifelong adaptation and particularly in adaptation in old age.

James and Marion Hanley have known each other most of their lives and have been married thirty-nine years. They both agree that their relationship has been by far the most important part of their lives.

They met in school. He was twelve and she was ten. They became friends and then sweethearts. When he was twenty-one and she was nineteen, they eloped. "I stole her from them." During the Depression, Mr. Hanley did not have a job. The two of them went from one farm to another, working in the fields. He finally got a job as a shoe repairman.

Four years after they married, their son was born. "I knew he could hear," Mrs. Hanley said, "because he was sleeping in his crib and Jim came in and dropped something. He woke up and started to scream. I didn't mind him screaming—I was happy [that he could hear]."

Two years later their daughter was born. A few months later, on the Fourth of July, Mrs. Hanley was sitting by the window while the baby slept, watching children play with fireworks. The firecrackers were so loud that Mrs. Hanley could hear them. The baby slept right through it. "I thought to myself, 'She must be deaf.' I wasn't disappointed; I thought, 'It will be all right. We are both deaf, so we will know what to do [how to communicate with her].'"

They moved around a lot when they lived in the Midwest. According to Mr. Hanley, "Work wasn't steady. It took that whole area a long time to recover from the Depression." He would hear about a job in some small town, and they would move there, often being the only deaf family in town. On Saturday nights they would bundle the children into the car and drive as far as a hundred miles to the nearest deaf club. Mrs. Hanley commented on the great distances they traveled during those years. She said, "It was lonely moving around like we did."

In 1956 they moved to California, settling in a South Bay suburb. Their two children have since married and had children of their own. Both children live with their families in a suburb about twenty-five miles away. "We drive over in our trailer most weekends and spend our time with them. Our whole family belongs to the deaf camping club, so we spend vacations together, too."

Mr. and Mrs. Hanley also spend a good deal of their time socializing with other deaf couples who live nearby. When they have the time they stay home and work on hobbies they share.

Mr. Hanley summarizes his feelings about their relationship when he says, "It's a pleasure to be with her. The first time I saw her I knew she was the one I wanted to go through life with, and I still feel that way."

Creating one's own family symbolizes acceptance of deafness. Within their own family circle deaf people resolve some of the ambivalence they have experienced about the disability since childhood and reaffirm their identity.

Most marriages among the elderly deaf have been enduring, on a par with the hearing cohort (Sussman, 1977). In old age these relationships are characterized by interdependence and mutual interests. The deaf elderly follow a pattern of joint conjugal-role relationships, described by Bott (1957), in which the husband and wife share many duties and spend much leisure time together. Bott found, however, that individuals who followed this pattern tended to be connected with others through a dispersed and heterogeneous network and were not members of a tightly knit social network. In contrast, the aged deaf, both as members of a group and as partners in conjugal-role relationships are maximizing those social relationships that have the greatest potential for meaningful interaction.

INTIMACY

Intimacy is one of the critical stages in Erikson's (1950) developmental schema and is an important personal resource in old age (Lowenthal et al., 1975). Weiss (1979) states that intimacy between spouses in old age is a buffer from the stresses accompanying the aging process. He found that "older people who had a high level of spouse intimacy did not display such a significant negative association between stress and adaptation." A high level of spouse intimacy has provided the support necessary to come to terms with deafness, the major stress of life, in early and middle adulthood. In later life, intimacy has been important in adapting to the stresses of aging.

During my fieldwork I interviewed twelve different couples. While interviewing them I observed two differing kinds of behavior. Eight of the twelve couples complemented each other, in the sense that there was give and take between them, and they shared equally in imparting information and answering questions. They consulted each other and had systems for getting each other's attention discreetly. At times they became so involved in each other that they seemed to forget I was there. Subsequent observation and interviews with them individually reinforced my initial impression that their marriages had a high degree of intimacy and mutual consensus. Mr. and Mrs. Hanley, described above, are such a couple. Mrs. Jensen says of couples in the deaf community, "The husband and the wife often think of each other as their best friend. I know many couples who have that kind of relationship."

In contrast to those who displayed a high degree of intimacy, I observed and interviewed four couples who had difficult relationships with each other. In each case they vied for my time, interrupted each other, argued, and behaved much more autonomously. They displayed a variety of problems in their marital relationships, including power struggles, unresolved difficulties over differing communication modes, and dependency conflicts. These conflicts were aggravated by the problems of old age.

CHILDREN

Deaf couples in the subsample had small families. The mean number of children was two per family. Fifty-nine, or 91 percent, of the sixty-five children born to people in this subsample are hearing. Children of deaf parents absorb their parents' values; reared in the deaf community, their first language is sign language, and their first allegiance is to the values of collectivity and interdependence.

Approximately 10 percent of deaf parents bear deaf children (Rainer et al., 1963:14). Membership in a deaf family provides ascribed status in the community. The combination of ascribed status and linguistic competence leads to eventual leadership roles in the deaf community. Deaf people from all-deaf families are the continuous thread in the transmission of the culture. The sense of continuity and consistency expressed by deaf children of deaf parents was in sharp contrast to the histories of those deaf individuals who had hearing parents.

Hearing children are the link with the hearing world and often help their parents develop closer ties with that world. The hearing children of deaf parents share some similarities with second-generation Americans. Immigrants experience ambivalence about their children taking on the new culture, but ultimately they must rely on their children to bridge the cultural and linguistic gap. Similar feelings of ambivalence are overridden in the deaf community by the knowledge that hearing children can become part of the outside world. Nevertheless, people worry that their children will grow away from the deaf community and thus from them. In old age the status of the adult child vis-à-vis the community is expressed through comments such as "she loves the deaf."

From the hearing child's point of view, his or her deaf parents may be a source of stigma. For example, in one case the hearing daughter of a deaf couple was an only child. There were no other deaf people in the neighborhood where she grew up, and consequently she was the only child in her school with deaf parents. She said that the other children teased her relentlessly. She went through a long period of being embarrassed about their signs, the way they sounded when they spoke, and the mistakes they made in English. In retrospect she says, "Really, my parents are very well educated for deaf people, and they look like respectable middle-class citizens. But I couldn't see it. They were the bane of my existence. When we went somewhere together, I would sit in another part of the bus and pretend I didn't know them. I must have hurt them a lot."

The need to rely on a person with normal hearing for certain transactions results in the use of children as interpreters. Children must often interpret for their deaf parents at a very early age, as young as three or four. This role requires children, usually the oldest child in each family, to accept unusually heavy responsibilities. For example, in one case a physician used a man's hearing daughter as an interpreter in order to tell him that his illness was terminal.

Parent-child interaction is influenced by variations in the ability of family members to use different modes of communication. Parents who use one mode of communication with each other and another for their interactions with their children can create divisions within the family. Mr. Slocum said, "I can't lip-read at all but my wife is a good lip-reader. She never signed to one of our children, just talked to her and read her lips. So what happens? My daughter and I can't communicate."

Another variation in family communication occurs in families in which each child develops a unique way of communicating with the parents. A woman with deaf parents said, "There are four of us kids, and each one of us communicates with our parents differently. For example, I can't understand my brother when he's talking to my mother. It's confusing, but we have always been able to work it out." These variations in communication have an effect on family sociability in old age.

RELATIONS WITH ADULT CHILDREN IN OLD AGE

As people age relations with their children continue to be an important part of social life. The quality and quantity of interaction between elderly deaf parents and their children's families varies considerably. Communication barriers influence the relationship between deaf parent and adult child as these barriers impinge on other relationships, such as the inability to communicate with one's son- or daughter-in-law or with one's grandchildren. Such communication problems affect the adaptive strategies the individual develops as he or she approaches old age.

The factor that most influenced parent-child relationships was the child's involvement in the deaf community. Hearing children who are employed as interpreters, teachers, or in other professions where they are in touch with the deaf community, and children who are deaf themselves, have the most contact with their parents when they reach adulthood. Among families such as these contact varies, some families seeing each other daily, others weekly. Parents and their children tend to live within a few miles of each other.

The deaf adult children of individuals in the subsample had close family relationships with their parents and siblings. Those who lived in the same geographic area lived in close proximity to their parents and participated in social events together, such as activities at the state school. Those who lived at great distances maintained their family ties in a variety of ways, one of which was through weekly long-distance conversations by TTY.

Much pride is taken in grandchildren who know sign language, for this symbolizes the grandparents' success in having taught the value of the culture to their own children. Lack of communication with one's grandchildren is a source of considerable bitterness for many aging deaf people. Mrs. Jeffers's grandchildren all know finger-spelling and sign language. When she told a group of women, they were all impressed. Mrs. James responded bitterly, "I can't communicate with my grandchildren at all."

Divorce sometimes results in the loosening of parental ties with children, traditionally ties between father and children (Bell, 1971:524). For the deaf elderly it puts additional strains on parent-child relationships. For example, Mr. Matthews said, "I don't see much of my kids anymore. My son and I can't communicate very well. He never learned much sign language. And my daughter—well, when we divorced, she took my ex-wife's side. But my ex-wife doesn't see much of her either."

Similar stories were repeated by all of the other divorced parents in the sample, with one exception. Mr. Richards' son works in the deaf community and continues to see his father regularly.

In general, it appears that the stigma attached to divorce a generation ago, added to the stigma of deafness and the difficulties of communication, proved too stressful for many parent-child relationships to survive.

DEPENDENCY IN OLD AGE

Many Americans fear dependency in old age because the American culture emphasizes independence. The aged deaf are no exception. Nevertheless, increasing infirmity often forces people to rely more and more on their adult children, particularly on their daughters, a pattern that predominates among the general population (Sussman, 1977:227). Blenkner (1969) calls this "filial maturity" and says that roles are not reversed per se, but change as a natural outcome of the growing maturity of adult children.

When deaf parents become unable to care for themselves and must move to live closer to their children, they usually spend increased time with their children's family, and their time with peers is decreased. Most adult children try to foster their parents' spirit of independence. Dependence may increase, however; hearing children have been interpreters for their parents since childhood, a role that reinforces an overdeveloped sense of responsibility.

SIBLING RELATIONSHIPS

In the United States, relationships with siblings take on added importance in old age. Lowenthal and Robinson (1977: 434) suggest that people seek out and renew sibling relationships in old age. Based on a study of sibling relationships, Cumming and Schneider (1962:501) state, "Generational solidarity seems to be a very important relational tie of the last twenty or thirty years of life." Among deaf people sibling relationships are often renewed as spouses and other kin die.

Communication between siblings in old age is often difficult among the deaf, despite the ability of many siblings to sign and finger-spell. The sister of a deaf woman said to me, "I envy your ability to talk to her with such ease. They [the deaf siblings] were away at school so much, we never really learned enough sign language." A deaf woman said that her sister with normal hearing never really learned to sign well enough to communicate with her until the other deaf and hearing family members had died and they were forced to depend on each other.

Despite complaints about the quality of communication, the feeling underlying most sibling relationships in old age was expressed by one informant this way: "My sister and I are the only ones left of eight children. We're all the family either of us has got, so we have to take care of each other." An adult child of deaf parents analyzed his parents' relationships with their siblings by saying, "It's not the quality or quantity of communication that's important—it's the family bonds. They hang out together—say hello, pantomime getting fat, then sit down and watch TV together. It's symbolic."

Communication barriers have a pervasive effect on the deaf family. They thwart interaction, not only with siblings, grandchildren, and in-laws, but sometimes with one's own children as well. Even those families who have experienced optimum relations within the nuclear family in young adulthood may be unable to establish bonds with the child's family of procreation later in life. The reaffirmation of peer relationships late in life is an adaptive response to the communication barriers that exist in the extended family. By focusing socially and emotionally on the peer group, the deaf individual is able to avert dependency on children while maintaining compensatory relationships. In the next three chapters I shall discuss the social life that has developed among the aged deaf, partly in response to these barriers in family communication.

VI

The Basis of
Social Organization

The deaf community has developed its own elaborate patterns of social interaction in response to the continual threat of isolation and difficulties in communication. These compensatory patterns are established in early childhood and are maintained throughout the life cycle. In this chapter I shall discuss the important role the peer group plays in the development of adaptive strategies.

A basis for social support is normally developed in childhood. In the United States, this basis is generally composed of one's parents, parents' friends, kin, and peers. Such avenues for social expansion are often closed to most deaf people, and consequently, they turn to peers from lack of other supports.

The development and continuation of the peer group in the deaf community is of particular interest to anthropologists because it differs from the predominant pattern of peer-group formation in the general population of the United States. In contrast to the American pattern of friendship formation that occurs in adolescence (Hurlock, 1967), the deaf child's peer group is formed at the time the child enters the institution or private school.[1] We may attribute early peer-group formation to the overall impact of the school experience on the deaf child.

The deaf person's relation to the peer group is striking because these primary relationships usually last sixty or more years, extending over the entire life cycle. Such long-term relationships are unusual in the United States today, where a pattern of mobility is the norm. Lifelong peer relationships occur cross-culturally, usually in nonindustrialized societies. Moore (1978) refers to them as "life-term social arenas."

The importance of the peer group for a deaf person varies in different periods of the life-span. Crucial early in life, it becomes less important in mid-life when people are rearing their families. Once children are grown, however, the peer group again achieves critical importance.

Pointing to a long table where twelve people were eating lunch, Mrs. Bianchi said,

> *"You see those people sitting over there? Those are my classmates from the Berkeley School. When I was nine, my mother took me out of the hearing boarding school and put me in the institution. They all befriended me, and we have been tight ever since. Of course, once we all started families we didn't always see each other as regularly as we do now that everyone is retired. It's hard on my husband—he's from out of state and didn't grow up with us, so he feels kind of left out."*

The peer group can provide many of the social and emotional needs people experience across the life-span. In addition to its potential for community formation and intimate

1. This pattern is true not only for the cohort under discussion but for all succeeding generations of deaf children up to the present. Until recent efforts began to provide deaf children with language in the first few years of life, the creation of peer groups generally took place simultaneously with language acquisition, at the age of five or six years.

relationships, the peer group provides a substitute for relationships with extended kin. The individual can rely on agemates for close relationships, social support, and a sympathetic ear for listening to and dealing with common problems. One of the most important needs the peer group fills for the deaf is the continuing need for socialization.

THE PEER LEARNING PROCESS

Although the focus of peer socialization in the literature has been primarily on childhood and adolescence, peer socialization is a process that continues throughout life (Brim and Wheeler, 1966). Margaret Mead (1970) states that ongoing socialization is an active part of adult life, while Rosow (1974) has gone one step further and suggests that individuals are socialized to old age. The extent to which such socialization occurs is undoubtedly related to the amount of time spent with age-mates. Among deaf people awareness and acceptance of oneself as old is a by-product of the peer learning process, an adaptive strategy that originated to meet more basic needs.

For deaf people the peer learning process diminishes the effects of the sensory and social deficit experienced by the deaf individual. The peer learning process has developed in response to the dearth of information readily available to hearing people from newspapers and friends. Peer learning has become a formalized mechanism for coping with the informational vacuum.

> *Mrs. Atkins slipped into her bus seat next to me and said, "Good morning. . . . What's the news?" When I apologized for not having anything new to tell her she said, "Well, I just glanced at the paper this morning—there was a drug raid in Oakland yesterday. That's about all."*

The emphasis on news is a direct outcome of the lifelong information lag that deaf people experience. It has been channeled and patterned in such a way as to have become an institutionalized part of life. For example, one form of greeting is the sign idiom for "good news." People share both personal and impersonal news at their social gatherings.

Didactic monologues among people with normal hearing are usually limited to special circumstances, such as the formal teaching situation. Within the deaf community didactic monologues are common. One of the ways deaf people receive and communicate information to others is through "telling,"[2] a form of didactic teaching that is continually used for relaying information.

Gossip clearly serves a social function related to the learning process. Deaf people depend on a variety of sources for information. Reliability is a desirable but impossible quality to maintain. When the details of a story are missing, people speculate, and rumor abounds.

Ultimately, peer learning facilitates socialization to the social patterns of old age (Rosow, 1974). The individual with little peer contact may be more insecure about what the aging process means for him or her and may perceive aging more negatively than the person with greater contact. In old age the peer group helps the individual develop an aging identity and provides feedback about the aging process.

RELIGIOUS AFFILIATIONS

Religious affiliation is an important consideration to many people, whether or not they are active churchgoers, and plays a part in how they perceive other people. Religious preference is often related to the formation and maintenance of cliques in adulthood. For example, people think of themselves as Catholics or as Lutherans. Their religious identity may affect whom they choose to become their friends and whom they allow to remain acquaintances. Most of the time, however, there is

2. Jacqueline Hynes Peterson analyzed the meaning of this behavior from her own observations, in a personal communication, 3 October 1977.

friendship across religious lines. The small size of the community and the frequent necessity of marrying across religious lines helps to diminish separatist tendencies. Religious lines also tend to blur as people attend churches other than their own in order to participate in the social life of the church. Mrs. Daniels says, "I'm not Catholic, but I go to the one that serves the deaf near me. They have good socials on Sunday afternoons."

In old age, as mobility decreases, church attendance also decreases. Several of the churches serving deaf people are located either in ghetto areas or at great distances from the homes of the parishioners. Consequently, one focus of social life becomes less accessible in old age.

VOLUNTARY ORGANIZATIONS AMONG THE DEAF

Voluntary associations are based on common interests and voluntary membership. They provide social nurturance to their members. The importance of voluntary associations to anthropologists lies primarily in their social integrative functions in both complex and tribal societies (Banton, 1968).

The deaf community is a subsociety of joiners. Throughout their lives they use voluntary associations to maximize sociability. This process begins early in life. State schools, with their separation from society and their emphasis on group activities, foster attitudes that promote voluntary associations. In the deaf community the process of becoming a joiner begins during the school experience, with participation in sports events and social activities, and continues into old age.

When Mr. Slocum was twenty-one he moved from Canada to Los Angeles in order to live in a warmer climate. He did not know anyone in Los Angeles, and he did not know American Sign Language. He got a job, and he started going to the deaf club after work. Soon he was learning the language, par-

ticipating in a bowling league, and dating women he met at the club. He eventually met his wife-to-be there, and after they were married the deaf club continued to be the center of their social life.

Most major cities in the United States have a deaf club. A deaf person from San Francisco can walk into such a club in any other major city and meet old friends, acquaintances, or at the very least, friends of friends. The deaf clubs across the United States provide the physical locus from which hundreds of social networks radiate.[3]

Mr. Hinton, who is referred to by his friends as "a real club man," said, "I don't like to be home by myself. I get lonely. There is always someone to talk to at the Deaf Club."

The question of intergenerational relationships comes up most frequently in relation to deaf clubs. Deaf people see the purpose of deaf clubs traditionally as meeting the major social needs of deaf persons over the age of eighteen. In recent years the age-integrated complexion of deaf clubs has changed for several reasons.

First of all, the introduction of drugs into clubs by young members has resulted in the exodus of older deaf people from clubs where drug use occurs.

Mr. Sadler said, "I like the young kids. Some of the old timers say the young deaf live in a different world; that they don't have much in common with them. They don't understand the pot-smoking. That doesn't bother me. What does bother me is the terrible ignorance I see—from spelling a

3. The networks of the deaf extend across the nation. There are a variety of newsletters, newspapers, and several magazines which impart news of recent events. One of the most important factors in maintaining the nationwide scope of the deaf community is the importance of keeping in touch through travel. Those who travel long distances by car visit friends en route, bringing news with them and taking news to disseminate in the local community.

*three-letter word to preventing pregnancy. Life in the institu-
tion doesn't prepare them for real life. We [older people] all
went through that, but we forget what being young is like."*

Second, the buildings that house deaf clubs, purchased
forty or fifty years ago by the deaf, are now in ghettos, and old
people are afraid to visit them at night. Most young people, on
the other hand, do most of their socializing in the evening.
Mrs. Daniels said, "It depends—everyone is different. Some
people like to associate with young people, others don't. If
you have deaf children or grandchildren you naturally have a
lot more contact. The big mixer is still an activity like a deaf
picnic."

In spite of differences in lifestyle, the aged deaf maintain an
active interest in younger deaf people and provide financial
support for them. For example, through their contributions to
deaf organizations, they sponsor and promote athletics for
young members and youth groups, and they continue to participate in the extracurricular activities of the state school.
Younger deaf leaders actively seek out and rely on this support. Since the time when the fieldwork for this study was
done, the aged have become a force to contend with in the deaf
community by withdrawing financial support when their
wishes are overlooked.

The life experiences of the elderly deaf are recognized by
some younger deaf people as a source of enrichment and education for children. On one occasion, a teacher brought her
class of twelve-year-olds to a senior center so that the elderly
deaf could talk to the children about their lives. When the children were seated, each person in turn told his or her life story,
which was followed by a discussion led by the teacher on the
themes that emerged, such as work, marriage, children, and
long life.

Despite considerable intergenerational contact, in old age
deaf people are increasingly age-segregated, as they were in

childhood. Age segregation is an organizing principle of sociability. People of the same cohort share the same problems and pleasures as well as a perspective that relates to their development over the life-span (Foner, 1975). Among the aged deaf, age solidarity is reflected in the ages of voluntary association members.

In old age deaf people continue to identify with the deaf community. Having dealt with the problems of deafness, however, they are increasingly concerned with age-related problems. Consequently, deaf aged turn more and more frequently to community-wide agencies serving the general population of old people to meet their needs. Miss Jennings said, "Five years ago there was nothing for older deaf people to do in this city. The deaf club was only open at night; there wasn't even a monthly social. Now there is plenty to do. I can see all my friends regularly. I'm not so lonesome anymore."

Deaf aged use "senior citizen" programs as the structure around which they plan their social life. They often begin to attend functions for senior citizens before they retire, going on their days off or before or after work. Whether or not they do attend functions earmarked for older deaf people, they tend to socialize with the same people anyway—at deaf clubs, at church, and in each other's homes. When they retire they are not cut off from the people with whom they already have meaningful relationships. Rather, the opportunity to socialize with peers is increased.

When they join senior citizen groups deaf people in their sixties are confronted with the difficulties that people older than themselves must face. Mrs. Simpson says, "As I talk to my friends I feel lucky I have energy and health. But then I start to think about the future. What will I do when I can't drive anymore? I guess I will have to sell my house."

Discussion of the concerns of old age result in heightened awareness of the aging process. Younger people become better able to relate to older ones, thus drawing together those that Neugarten (1974) refers to as the young-old and the old-old. This process of group redefinition strengthens the mutual support system.

As this process occurs, aging identity is forged. It is a significant identity transformation and affects subsequent social interaction patterns. For the first time since childhood, the individual sees himself or herself as part of a subgroup within the deaf community. New bonds are created between individuals who formerly shared few interests. As they tell each other about their concerns a new theme begins to emerge—aging.

In old age most deaf people join various voluntary organizations serving the aged deaf, in contrast to Bultena's (1968) finding that voluntary association activities tend to decrease with increasing age. As the members of the group age they tend to meet less frequently in each other's homes. While visiting between homes continues to be an important part of life for people in their sixties, it becomes more and more difficult for people in their seventies and eighties to move around the dispersed deaf community. Thus, many people rely on long days of intensive social interaction several times a month in central locations to meet their social needs. I shall discuss this patterned social interaction in greater detail in chapter seven.

VIII

Social Relationships

The social patterns the deaf develop throughout their lives yield their rewards in old age. At a time when most Americans experience the shrinking of their social worlds (Rosow, 1974), the intensive quality of social life among the aged deaf creates a web of close or primary group relationships that sustains the individual in sickness and in health. In the following pages I shall discuss the ways in which social relationships provide adaptive strategies for aging.

Social relationships are important for personal growth. The wealth of social relationships among the deaf aged have helped to achieve considerable social and psychological integration for the individual by late life.

SOCIAL RITUALS

Social rituals invariably revolve around a society's institutions, underlining the importance of the institutions to the culture. In the deaf community social rituals have developed around friendship.

The major social institution in the deaf community is the deaf "social." A typical social I attended takes place monthly in a recreation building in the middle of a large park. This Bay Area city park is centrally located near a downtown shopping area. Nearby rapid transit and a freeway provide easy access. The park borders on a black ghetto, and children from the neighborhood attend a preschool that is connected with the recreation center by a corridor.

On the third Wednesday of each month, about 10:00 A.M., deaf people become visible in the area as they meet friends, signing to each other as they walk through the park. They are a well-dressed, attractive-looking group of people. Women wear pantsuits or dresses with wool coats or jackets. Most men wear sports jackets and slacks with white shirts and ties or open-necked shirts.

At 10:30 the doors are thrown open to a considerable crowd, and by 10:45 most of the hundred or more people who will attend this social are present. People move through the doors, stop to chat with the doorkeeper and pay their twenty-five cents in dues, then move on to greet each other enthusiastically with hugs and flurries of signs.

The recreation center consists of one large room set up like a school cafeteria, with tables pushed end to end to create rows, and with folding chairs set up at the tables. People bring their own lunches. As they greet their special friends they go together to put their lunches down where they plan to sit. Except for the very old and infirm, however, no one sits down just then. They all move busily around the room greeting each other and talking animatedly in a series of short encounters. There is an occasional shriek or shout as an old friend from out-of-town appears. Mostly, however, there is a low hum that accompanies the fifty or more conversations that are going at the same time.

Deaf socials are happy, lively occasions permeated by humor. The emphasis on different aspects of social conversation such as wit, storytelling, and debate, is directly related to the emphasis placed on face-to-face communication. When people worked they saved up their anecdotes and stories and looked forward to the weekend, when they would socialize at the deaf club. This pattern prevails in old age, and a cheerful joking attitude pervades the atmosphere. For example, Mr. Chase greeted me, "Hi, Gay, long time no see. [hug] Say, I like your new dress. Did you get it at Monkey's [Montgomery Ward's]?"

The period of active socializing continues during the morning. Common topics at socials include hobbies, travel, health, children and grandchildren, transportation, food, plans for the future, and mutual reminiscence. The public nature of this setting was underlined by Mr. Baker one day when he said to me, "How many conversations can you see and understand from here? I can see six different ones." Although people do discuss intimate subjects in this setting, lack of privacy prevents people from discussing topics that they do not want others to know about. If two people wish to talk privately, they either go to the bathroom or they use various techniques to hide what they are saying, such as using small signs while standing behind a pillar.

At noon people sit down either with their closest friends or with their childhood peers, who are sometimes one and the same. Coffee is provided by the recreation department. A cake is made at the deaf-school kitchen and brought to the social by a deaf leader who helped to start the group fourteen years ago.

As people eat they continue to talk, often carrying on signed conversations with others two tables away. During lunch the volunteers, deaf women in their forties and fifties, come around with tickets and coffee cans full of money. The tickets are for the raffle that is held at the annual Christmas party and for the discount on the price of the Christmas party meal. The party is held in a restaurant or hall big enough to accommodate the two hundred people who annually attend.

When lunch is over, people continue to sit and talk while they wait for the announcements. Mrs. Baker, a deaf woman who has been appointed leader by her peers, stands on a box at one end of the hall and waves her arms for attention. Several minutes pass before everyone notices her and stops talking. While she is waiting for their attention she talks to different people in the audience in a joking manner about how difficult it is to get their attention.

Mrs. Baker conducts the announcements in an informal and informative way. She starts out by joking with the audience— they would rather talk, talk, talk than watch her. Then she looks at her notes and delivers a short announcement, such as "Mrs. White fell and broke her hip last Saturday. If you would like to write to her, she is staying with her daughter, whose address is —————." If everyone already knows about Mrs. White, Mrs. Baker goes on to the next announcement. If not, she answers questions from the audience and leads a discussion about the details of the accident.

Once Mrs. Baker has the audience's attention, they are alert and involved. The announcement format insures that everyone is kept abreast of all relevant community events as well as news of specific individuals. When Mrs. Baker finishes her announcements, other members of the group are welcome to make their own, which are usually about community events.

After the announcements, a group picture is taken of all those who have birthdays during the month. The rest of the afternoon is devoted to cards, usually whist or Bingo, and talking.

Storytelling usually takes place in the afternoon among those who choose not to play cards. People arrange their chairs in a big circle. If more than twenty members of both sexes are present, it is likely that two circles will form, one for men and one for women.

One afternoon Mr. Crowthers told the following joke:

A man decided to try to tame wild beasts with violin music, so he went on an African safari. He took his violin and walked

*out into the bush. The first lion stalked him, then went away
as he played furiously; the second lion did the same. Along
came a third lion, and the man fiddled like mad. But the third
lion attacked. Why? He was deaf—he couldn't hear the
violin!*

In the "privacy" of the deaf social, where few hearing people
are present, deaf men sign their stories and jokes in big bold
signs, while the women look on. Many, but not all, of these
stories are about deafness.

In small groups, both men and women participate in storytelling and debate, covering a great variety of topics. Sometimes they engage in repartee. For example, I recorded the following field notes after one session:

*Then they talked about deaf animals—a long conversation
with much laughter. Mrs. Dennis said, "White cats with
blue eyes are deaf." Mr. Bauer responded, "Sometimes dogs
are deaf that have the same color fur and eyes." Then they
recounted all the deaf animals they had ever known personally
(i.e., pets). Mr. Bauer told two deaf animal stories—I wish I
could remember the punch lines.*

Another type of storytelling is the dramatization of events
that have happened to the individual or to some "character" in
the deaf community. Some of the stories have been repeated
many times, such as those told about Douglas Tilden, a well-
known sculptor of the early twentieth century who was deaf.

As the afternoon wanes the group begins to break up. At
3:00 o'clock Mrs. Baker flicks the lights and waves her arms.
"Out, out, you have to leave. Go home!" People wander out
slowly, talking to each other and joking with Mrs. Baker about
letting them stay. People continue to stand around and talk
after the doors are shut, finally moving off slowly into the
park.

The deaf social is a prime example of the normalization process at work. The term *normalizing* has been used to describe aspects of chronic illness and disability. In this context *normalizing* refers to a strategy of social interaction limited to given social situations. For example, Davis (1963) used the term in analyzing the social behavior of children with polio, and Strauss (1975:8) discusses normalizing in terms of disease management. In other words, normalizing is situational. Everyone experiences the need to normalize in some social situation at one time or another.

The concept of normalization as I use it covers a much broader area of behavior. Generally speaking, normalization is a process that occurs in all cultures to render everything logical. The normalization process occurs on all levels of consciousness *over time*. Normalization affects one's behavior as well as one's world view.

When the individual is continually reminded of his or her variance from others, this increases the level of stress and adversely affects behavior. Stress can best be minimized by playing down the overt differences of the disability and thus its importance. Among a tightly knit reference group, such as the deaf elderly, the effort to normalize will take place on a group as well as on an individual level. Thus, in the deaf social described above, everyone takes pains to be well-groomed in terms of the larger American middle-class society.[1] The emphasis is on harmony and good-natured fun. In this segregated setting the problems of coping with the disability are forgotten or dealt with by joking.

Normalization is a process that is not limited to deafness, or even to disability, although I shall discuss it primarily in these terms. It can occur within any disenfranchised group in a cul-

1. Myerhoff (1978a:142) notes that people whose lives are determined largely by forces beyond their control may be preoccupied with "face"; at the same time, they may generate internal codes for measuring each other in order to avoid the censure of society.

ture that is set apart by deviance or social marginality. It is likely that the larger the group, the younger the people, and the greater their shared sense of uniqueness, the more thorough the process will be. A group such as the aged deaf, who have been undergoing this process most of their lives, epitomizes the process at its most thorough.

Normalization is basically an in-group process. Introduction of outsiders into the group invites cognitive dissonance. As I mentioned earlier in discussing my fieldwork, people were initially reticent to talk to me. As a hearing person I was a threat to their feelings of normality. Outsiders are reminders that the world is not necessarily the way it is perceived by the in-group. For this reason, the in-group seldom accepts outsiders who are not deaf and hence do not possess the collective symbol of the group. Even the adult child of deaf parents who is a native signer is on the margin of the group if he or she can hear.

Among the deaf social awareness reaffirms relationships and group identification. The act of meeting and greeting in itself becomes a ritual that involves considerable time and attention. Failure to imbue a greeting with the proper degree of relational acknowledgment, such as whether to hug or to shake hands, is considered either insulting or ignorant. People both demand from and give attention to others in proportion to their perception of the relationship. Mithun (1973:32–33) discussed this same reification ritual as an adaptive mechanism among blacks.

In addition to the social round of regular activities, deaf people invest considerable energy in special events. During the year I was in the field the biggest celebration was the fiftieth wedding anniversary party of a popular couple in the community. One year before the event, a planning committee was formed under the direction of the couple's best friends. The committee was made up of thirty-three close friends, who made all the plans and reservations, sent the invitations, and paid for the basic costs of the party to be divided thirty-three ways. The party was held in a hotel at a local airport so that out-of-towners could easily come and go. Three hundred people attended this formal party, to which women wore floor-length dresses. Individuals paid for their own dinners and drinks. In a banquet room the guests socialized and drank for two hours, then sat down to a chicken dinner, which was followed by speeches honoring the anniversary couple. The party was a great success and the focus of much talk and discussion, both before and after the event.

I asked an informant who was on the committee if she had participated in other such planning efforts. She said, "Oh, yes, that is the usual way to put on a big party. I have been involved in a number of them over the years."

Ostensibly an anniversary party, this social occasion, like many others, was really a rite of reaffirmation. The act of socializing has an integrative function in keeping group members together. The social occasion becomes a display of solidarity. In order to maximize its success, as many people as possible must be involved in the preparation and carrying out of the event. These individuals share common knowledge about hosting such an event, generate enthusiasm, and keep others vicariously involved in planning. After the event many hours are spent in mutual reminiscence, further reaffirming the worth of the group and of the individual.

The importance of this type of social participation is underlined by the cost involved. American attitudes about the value of things are directly related to cost. American expressions of speech such as "Money talks" or "Put your money where your mouth is" indicate that talk is cheap, whereas money signifies commitment.

In the deaf community the commitment is to sociability, which, cumulatively, can be expensive. The cost of the anniversary dinner was eight dollars per person, not including drinks. For this and other social occasions it is impolite to say "I can't afford to go." Such a statement implies that the group is not worth the cost.

Social interaction develops and strengthens the bonds of the group. Interaction is also designed to strengthen the individual's identification with the group, and reflects positively on individual self-image. Miller (1963) says of this process, "The greater their weight as a reference group, the closer the public esteem is to the self-esteem and the more motivated the individual is to conform to the group's pressures" (p. 696).

Group identification is an important component of the adaptive behavior aged deaf people exhibit. They are more dependent on group identification than are people who are not deaf. They reconcile their identities as deaf people in the social arena, for it is in these settings that they have developed positive feelings of self-esteem. Thus, group identification provides the necessary balance to compensate for the negative aspects of deaf identity. It is this more than any other single factor which enables deaf people to develop integrated identities.

FRIENDSHIP PATTERNS

In American culture people disproportionately select friends who are in social positions similar to the ones they hold themselves (Fischer et al., 1977). This is certainly true of the deaf elderly; however, there is considerable social interaction between people of differing social statuses. Within the community social status is pervasive and implicit. Status becomes explicit only under certain circumstances, vis-à-vis the outside world.

Most older deaf people think of the majority of people in their cohort as friends. The small size of the group contributes to this feeling of group-wide friendship. For this reason, differences that inhibit social interaction in the larger society, such as ethnicity, class, and sex, are frequently ignored.

Friendship patterns among the aged deaf are based on the couple, as Babchuk (1965) observed in his sample of middle-class Americans. Mrs. Simpson said, "When my husband died, I was the only widow in the group. I often feel like a third wheel. But they are our lifelong friends, people we grew up with, so I tag along, and it's getting easier." Friendships in the deaf community are initiated by either partner. Friends of both sexes are almost invariably recruited from the peer group of childhood or young adulthood. While intimates are invariably of the same sex, many close friendships exist between men and women in the group. Mr. Bauer and Mrs. Gray, for example, have been close friends since they first went to school together. Single individuals tend to have their closest friends among the same sex, though they socialize with both sexes.

PRIMARY RELATIONS

One of the most important findings to come out of the gerontological literature in recent years is the role of primary relations in old age. Arth (1961:168) defines a close relationship as being one "between two persons, not kin, involving deep feelings of personal liking, trust, confidence, and dependability in time of crisis." Mrs. Simpson said of her best friend, "Of all my friends, I am closest to May. I can trust her, and she is completely dependable." Relationships of this type obviously have great significance for the individual in the development and maintenance of self-esteem.

Personal adjustment is related to primary-group support (Wilensky, 1961:236). This factor has positively affected the life adjustment of the deaf. Aging deaf individuals average five or six close friends. In contrast, Babchuk (1965:483) states that the modal number of close friends in the United States is two. The difference in numbers alone of primary-group relationships ensures a supply of meaningful interaction in old age.

Relationships intertwine in complex social networks. A socially active person may have more than one set of primary relationships, which may, in turn, overlap each other.

CLIQUES

The development of intense, overlapping relationships is related to the development of cliques. Cliques—usually of about six people—are widespread in the deaf community. They are based on a combination of factors, including mode of communication, school ties, ethnicity, religion, geographic proximity, degree of education, and mutual interests. Although mode of communication is the most frequent factor determining the make-up of a clique, the other factors are also important. For example, one clique is composed of orally raised individuals who live in the same geographic area, while another clique is made up of Italian manualists who live at considerable distance from one another.

The clique may help the individual adjust to a new situation—for example, Navajos who migrated to Denver adjusted to their new environment with the help of cliques (Snyder, 1973). The atmosphere of the deaf clique is conducive to discussions of problems of living. Mrs. Dennis said, "Every Tuesday the six of us get together for lunch and cards. We talk and talk. What about? Oh, you know—our families, what happened yesterday—life, I guess." The clique may also fulfill an important role in helping the individual make life adjustments; for example, clique contact is an important part of ongoing socialization to aging.

SECONDARY RELATIONSHIPS

The overlapping social ties within the group and the public nature of communication mean that everyone knows everyone else and has considerable knowledge about the lives of most other people. In addition to the importance of primary ties, secondary relationships are also important. They are activated when primary-group members are unavailable.

> *Mrs. Parsons, whose close friends are all dead, looked delighted when she spotted Miss Jennings at a deaf social. As the two women headed for each other, Mrs. Parsons said, "I taught her sign language when she first came to the deaf club. We have known each other for many years."*

Secondary relationships, significant throughout people's lives, attain particular significance in old age. As the community decreases in size, through death and immobility, those remaining must rely increasingly on secondary relationships to fulfill their social and emotional needs. These relationships, which have demonstrated strength and endurance, are thus able to take over many of the functions of the former primary relationships.

NEIGHBORS

Neighborliness is a valued commodity in American life. Neighbors become especially important in old age, when the individual becomes more restricted physically. Rosow (1970: 58) states that neighbors become more important than friends in old age.

Of 43 households in the subsample 19 had one deaf neighbor or more, and 12 were located near relatives, either siblings or children. In addition, most people know their hearing neighbors. Mrs. Jensen said of one friend, "We were neighbors for twenty-five years. She took care of me whenever I was sick. It gave me such security knowing she was there." Neighborliness in urban areas is as variable for deaf people as it is for everyone else. Undoubtedly, the most important thing provided by neighbors in old age is a sense of security. For many people neighbors fill in the gaps that may exist in the individual's social support system.

RECIPROCITY

Reciprocity and exchange theory has long been a concern of students of social processes. Reciprocity plays a special role as a mechanism of adaptive behavior. The study of reciprocal relationships among Samoan-Americans, for example, has demonstrated the important role of mutual aid in the process of adaptation to urban life (Ablon, 1971). A discussion of the role that reciprocity plays in the lives of the aged deaf follows.

Patterns of reciprocity have developed that are specifically geared to the needs of the aged deaf. Reciprocity is most often related to the exchange of services and personal attention, and less frequently to the exchange of goods; for example, one of Mr. Ciano's best friends installed the light attached to his doorbell for him.

Mutual aid is an important part of social life in the deaf community. The feelings of mutuality that are shared by deaf people reinforce the importance of mutual aid. Mutual aid takes many forms and occurs most often among neighbors and close friends. One day when I was visiting Mrs. Chase, Mr. Taylor appeared with two tickets to the county fair. When he left, Mrs. Chase gave him a sample of a new recipe she had just made to share with his wife when he got home.

In contrast to the increased importance of telephones (Dignum, 1979) and public transportation for most older people, the cliché in the deaf community, "My car is my phone," assumes new significance in old age. Staff members at a local senior center have observed that deaf people continue to drive at a greater age than do hearing people. People who have cars transport those who can no longer use public transportation to the various social events. Mrs. Parsons said, "I'd die of loneliness if the Jacksons didn't bring me to the different socials." As people grow older and less mobile, assistance with transportation becomes more and more important in their lives. Failure to provide transportation for frail people who live nearby is met with censure.

Tangible forms of aid such as the loan of money do take place between close friends, but people do not talk about it. Financial affairs are generally a well-kept secret because of the lack of privacy in the group. By old age most people have learned to be careful with their money. If a person must borrow money, he or she will borrow from his or her adult child or from a best friend.

Reciprocation also extends outside of the group itself for services provided. For example, volunteered interpreting services for a group are paid for by passing a hat.

Perhaps the most important kind of mutual aid is the group support that people can count on in time of crisis. This is true for both short-term and long-term crises. Group support is a viable, sustaining force that helps individuals deal with all kinds of problems. It brings together people who have little in common.

Long-term group support is most apparent with serious illness. For example, when Mr. Gerardi's wife was ill with cancer, each time her husband got up to leave a group meeting everyone signed, "Give her our love," then flashed the sign for "I love you" as he walked out the door. Whenever Mrs. Gerardi felt well enough to join the group, she was welcomed with delight and surrounded by people who wanted to greet her and talk to her.

The group support enabled Mr. and Mrs. Gerardi to continue their social life without the ostracism often experienced by cancer patients and their families. At the same time, it strengthened group identification and helped people cope with their feelings about her illness through group discussion.

Social supports such as those described in this chapter enhance individual functioning in old age. The social processes that are integral to these relationships are complex, and for this reason I shall discuss them separately in chapter eight.

VIII

Social Processes

The normalizing efforts of the deaf require continual face-to-face interaction with a sizable group of deaf peers. The existence of the support group for purposes other than normalizing, such as reciprocity, emotional support, and substitute relationships, helps to forestall the impact of age-linked losses. In this chapter I shall discuss the social processes that have arisen out of deaf social behavior, and their role in maintaining these adaptive strategies.

As I stated in chapter seven, the normalization process is a group process, and there must be cooperation among the ranks for it to take place. Thus, when a group such as the deaf has strong values related to social behavior, the individual must internalize these values in order to adapt successfully to his or her disability. The less one shares certain values with others, the more problems one will have in normalizing.

Mr. Emmett Bailey, a sixty-eight-year-old man, does not have a strong sense of group identification and consequently has continual difficulty in normalizing. In the context of his peer group he is a misfit. Mr. Bailey does not like to socialize. He says it is a waste of time. "I have too many important things to do to spend my time with the deaf."

Mr. Bailey has never devoted much time to sociability with his deaf peers. He married in his early twenties, and he and his wife had two children. During the time the children were growing up Mr. Bailey seldom visited the deaf club or participated in community events. "What do I want to be bothered with all that for? I don't like to gossip and sit about." When his children married and left home, he and his wife were divorced. "We had drifted apart. We had nothing to say to each other."

Since that time Mr. Bailey has become active in his church, where he interacts primarily with hearing church members. He has taken a variety of adult education classes and recently enrolled in a junior college to study computer technology. He took a woodworking class at a local senior center and participated for several months, until some other deaf people joined the class, at which point he dropped out.

When Mr. Bailey does appear at a deaf social, others politely acknowledge him, exchange a few words of greeting, then resume whatever they were doing. He has membership in the group because he grew up with them; he went to the state school and married another member of the deaf community. He is blunt about his negative feelings for other deaf people, however, and in turn, they are cool to him.

Mr. Bailey admits to being lonely. His need to be the "token" deaf person prevents him from establishing long-term relationships with people. His failure to use the coping mechanisms of his peers has resulted in an isolated lifestyle.

The values shared by the aged deaf derive from their deaf identity: being deaf is the single most important factor in their lives: one owes allegiance to deafness; and one must further the good of the community, putting it before oneself if necessary. The outcome of sociability is seen as the perpetuation of the community. Simultaneously, deaf identity is reinforced.

These values rely not only on a philosophical point of view

but on action as well. If the individual does not really believe in the importance of putting deafness—and thus sociability and all of its symbolic meaning—first for group well-being, then he or she will pursue other activities. Detachment from these values will be noted by others, and the normalization process will be thwarted.

The cost of risk-taking for people who are marginal to the larger society provides incentive for people to internalize the values of the group. The disabled status requires deaf people to spend more time working out their relationship with the world and less time on their own inner development.

Conformity to a group norm serves important functions, especially for those who must continually deal with their own nonconformity. Conformity decreases feelings of deviance and, at the same time, heightens feelings of belongingness, a process that occurs both consciously and unconsciously. This process is related to deviance disavowal. Davis (1961) used this term in discussing the response of nonstigmatized individuals' behavior toward the stigmatized. As part of the normalization process, however, the aged deaf dissociate themselves from others who suffer from a different social stigma: minority group members, the socially deviant, and those with other disabilities.

Values relating to the importance of the group's well-being underlie the ways in which social control is enforced.

SOCIAL PRESSURE

In a group such as the deaf, which has a restricted communication field and a limited number of people, social pressures to conform will be great. Within the deaf community, failure to conform to the strong, positive value attached to sociability and group participation results in the application of considerable social pressure, such as "nagging" and gossip.

By far the most consistent social pressures have to do with

the individual's behavior in regard to group participation. The continual threat of having the group's numbers decimated by illness and death prompts the group to encourage full participation in old age. Mrs. Daniels remarked, "People expect me to go to everything, and I just can't do it. I don't have the energy to be constantly on the go like I used to."

Social pressure to participate is kept up regardless of the frequency of contact an individual maintains. When a social occasion is looming ahead, everyone asks, "Are you going?" or "You will be there, won't you?" The continual one-to-one social pressure clearly displays approval or displeasure.

When an individual does not participate fully in group activities, that person is called standoffish or snobbish. Absence activates gossip and criticism. Ostracism is not practiced, because the group needs all participants. Failure to participate, except in cases of illness, results in a growing coolness on the part of group members.

The relationship between social pressure and group identification is clear. It is felt that the individual either does or does not identify with the social meaning of being deaf. His or her lack of participation is seen as illustrating a lack of identification and therefore is a negative comment about the worth of the group.

One of the most frequently used kinds of social pressure is gossip. Gossip fulfills several functions. First of all, gossip is a very effective means of social control, as in all groups (Gluckman, 1963). People reconsider potential action because of the gossip one's actions might provoke. This is not to suggest that all behavior is externally directed. Internal controls are an important check on behavior, especially in old age. Perhaps it would be more accurate to say that gossip curtails inaction and encourages interaction.

Second, gossip is social glue. Although people dread being gossiped about, they continue to gossip about others. Gossip provides subjects of mutual interest and serves the peer informational functions discussed earlier. The more exclusive the group, the greater will be the amount of gossip it produces. When a group has exclusiveness thrust upon it, through isolation, for example, its potential for gossip will be the greatest.

RESOLVING CONFLICT WITHIN THE GROUP

Conflict that occurs within the group threatens the group's functioning. If conflict is not controlled, it may undermine the whole fabric of group life by disturbing the patterns of sociability. Given a limited number of people with whom they can communicate and no other group to whom they can turn, deaf individuals usually work toward keeping in-group conflict under control.

The close proximity in which the aged deaf go through life together insures that conflict will arise. When it does arise, it is either caused by or channeled into specific areas that are related to language: (1) communication and (2) the constant controversy between oralists and manualists.

COMMUNICATION

Language is symbolic of conflict for older deaf people, with their long history of language-related aggravations (see chapter three). In old age communication is laden with a lifetime of emotionally charged experiences. Difficulties in communication arouse a range of social insecurities, as well as emotional responses such as feelings of stigma, guilt, and ambivalence. When misunderstandings occur, the problematical nuances of social interaction are attributed to the traditional troublemaker, the language.

ORALISTS AND MANUALISTS

When Americans do not get along, they often attribute it to self-defined boundaries, such as ethnicity or religion. When deaf people do not get along, they usually attribute it to factors related to the oral-manual controversy. In the process individuals reaffirm their own identity, as in "I think the oralists may have better manners, but they're a small bunch compared with us."

In interpreting the conflict of others, the oral-manual controversy is often given as the reason for conflict. For example, Mr. Matthews commented that Mrs. Daniels and her sister, who lives in another state, do not get along because "she was raised as a manualist and her sister was raised as an oralist." When I interviewed Mrs. Daniels later, she told me that she and her sister do not get along because they are very competitive. They share the same communication mode, however.

This example reflects the way in which problems are attributed to certain symbolic motifs of life in the deaf community. Further, it reflects the use of these motifs in the resolution of conflict.

Informal means of social control work very well to produce conformity within the homogeneous group. The mechanisms used work only within the cohort, however. Methods of social control become less effective when other age groups of deaf people are involved.

In the preceding pages I have discussed some of the means by which adaptive strategies are anchored in the life of the group. In the next chapter I shall discuss how such lifelong behavior prepares the individual to deal with the end of life.

IX

Facing Death

Friends are important, not only to share leisure activities, but also for support in serious concerns, such as facing death. In this chapter I shall discuss how adaptive strategies that revolve around friendship sustain people to the end of life.

DEALING WITH DEATH

In the United States, death, in theory if not in reality, happens only to old people. Age influences our perceptions about death. As we grow older the deaths of others—parents, friends, kin—become increasingly frequent. At the same time, the aging process affects how we perceive our own eventual death. In effect, the anticipation of death in old age is an organizer of time (Kalish, 1977:486). That is, old people perceive future time differently from the way young people do.

In American society, surveys about attitudes toward death show that people fear the death of others more than they fear their own (Geer, 1965). By the time they are in their sixties most deaf people have experienced the death of their parents, a sibling, or a close friend, and often the death of one's spouse or child. The death of others and one's own inevitable death have become an ever-present reality, a theme that recurs again and again in conversation. The death of a group member stirs up individual concerns and precipitates discussion. There was considerable expression of fear of death among the aged deaf; the concerns they expressed, however, were primarily related to the process of death itself and the meaning of the individual's death for the group.

DISENGAGEMENT

Deaf individuals in this study tended to express less fear about death the older they were. An attitude of calm acceptance was not apparent, however, except among some of the people over eighty years of age. Disengagement, a theory that hypothesizes that individuals detach themselves emotionally from relationships with others preparatory to dying (Havighurst, Neugarten, and Tobin, 1968:161), does not apply to the aged deaf. Only one person in the subsample appeared to be withdrawing from her peers. She was over eighty years of age, and all of those with whom she had had primary relationships were dead.

The other six people in the subsample in their eighties all maintained some primary-group relationships and did not exhibit any indications of disengagement. Mr. Wilson at eighty is beginning to make some minor adjustments to his age. Before he left on his summertime auto trip to Alaska, he commented that it would probably be the last time he drove there.

How do the deaths of significant others relate to one's impending sense of death? Significant relationships may be the vital forces that keep people from becoming disengaged. If so, it explains why the model of disengagement has little relevance for the aged deaf.

DEATH AS A PROCESS

Much more common than the fear of death itself is the fear that one will die and that things "will not go right." Deaf people have two related fears about this problem. First, they fear dying and not being found right away. This is a fear experienced by many hearing people who live alone. Deaf people, however, fear that their communication problems will somehow transcend their death and interfere with orderly burial procedures.

During my fieldwork, the death of a woman in the community was actually surrounded with such confusion. The finding of her body was recounted, and the importance of leaving instructions to relatives or friends in a prominent place was emphasized to the group at a large get-together. Later that week I visited an informant and saw a sign placed on the mantel, which read: "If happen dead or injured, contact my son, John Neal, at ———." Mrs. Neal explained that dying alone had happened to her friend, so it could happen to her.

Second, people fear that in death they will lose control because of their deafness, as they have in life. Mrs. Chase greeted me at the door one day with this: "Did you know that Allen Markley died? The funeral was yesterday. I read it in the paper just now. Why didn't his children let us know? He was my husband's best friend." Most people instructed their hearing relatives to get in touch with their deaf friends in the case of their death. Thus, the potential for conflict between one's hearing family members and one's deaf peers is present to the end.

MOURNING PATTERNS

People are concerned about the details of death. The death and dying process tends to follow two patterns: one pattern when a person dies suddenly and another when a person has a lingering illness.

Mrs. Gerardi was seriously ill for a long time. Her friends talked about it continually. They took turns keeping her husband company each time she was hospitalized. When she died, little was said about her actual death. Instead, people discussed the details of her funeral.

In contrast, when Mrs. Moore died suddenly, speculation

was rampant as to the circumstances under which she died. Many people approached me to ask if I knew what "really" happened. They would then discuss the new information among themselves. This process of questioning and discussing alleviates individual anxieties about one's own death and enables people to undergo the grieving process. After a long group discussion of Mrs. Stanley's death, one of her friends commented, "I feel so sad. It helps to talk about it."

THE MEANING OF DEATH FOR THE GROUP

When a person dies, his or her death affects the group to the extent that the individual has been active in the group. The number of people that attend a funeral depends on the popularity of the individual and the length of time it takes to spread the word. Mr. Dennis was a popular leader in his mid-seventies. When he died, over a hundred people attended his funeral, all members of the deaf community; when Mrs. Moore, an eighty-year-old widow, was buried, only about twenty deaf people and twenty hearing relatives were at her funeral.

Regardless of the number of people at the funeral, each individual's death has an impact on the group. Mr. Matthews pointed to a recent photo he had taken of the group and said to me, "Look how many are gone. The group is getting smaller and smaller. Awful!"

As a group, the aged deaf are aware of the need to try to fill the gap the dead person has left in the lives of spouses and best friends. At such times friends are a source of comfort. When Mr. Murray's wife died, his best friend began to accompany him everywhere daily.

Group members expressed distress whenever a schoolmate from the same class died, whether or not they were close to the person. When Mrs. Moore heard of the death of a classmate, she said, "They're all gone now except me and a girl up in Santa Rosa. I can hardly believe it." The deaths of members of the original peer group emphasized the individual's own sense of mortality.

When the best friend or the last of the clique dies, the system of coping that the individual has developed begins to deteriorate. Although the loss of one's friends is grievous, most individuals display a capacity to adapt to the situation by seeking out new friends from among their secondary relationships. This flexibility assures people of continual meaningful relations with peers.

From the preceding discussion it is apparent that individual deaths have a profound effect on the group. The importance of working out one's own mortality and of reaffirming the relationship with the deceased is part of the process of letting go of the person who has died.

This process is eased if the bereaved individual has a large peer group with whom he or she can (1) work through the emotional impact of the loss through discussion and interaction, and (2) establish other compensatory relationships to make up for the loss to some degree. This opportunity for self-expression heightens one's sense of well-being in old age.

The way that the aged deaf cope with death contrasts dramatically with the patterns of avoidance and denial of death that Byrne (1974) observed in studying a retirement community. While the deaf, because of their tight-knit relationships, are forced to confront death frequently, the lack of such long-term relationships in most age-segregated settings makes death an ever-present reality for which there are no adequate coping mechanisms.

X

Adaptation to Old Age

Becoming human is becoming individual, and we become individual under the guidance of cultural patterns, historically created systems of meaning in terms of which we give form, order, point, and direction to our lives.

Interpretation of Cultures
CLIFFORD GEERTZ (1973:52)

This study is concerned with group formation among people with a lifelong disability. The aged deaf, defined by the larger society as afflicted, have created a small society that has had an influence throughout life on both their disability and the perception of old age. Individuals in this specially created society have used group membership to achieve a nonstigmatized personal identity and normalized social relationships. These factors stand them in good stead throughout the life cycle. It is when they become old, however, that these factors are especially useful in coping with late life.

MANIPULATION OF THE SOCIAL ENVIRONMENT

Innovation is the basis of cultural change. When existing patterns of behavior are not functional and alternatives arise, the potential for change occurs.

As cultural differentiation takes place changes become institutionalized. Cultures adapt to changed circumstances in this way. Similarly, groups of marginal people make changes to accommodate their marginality. For example, the cultural view of disability differs from the disabled person's self-perception. In order to diminish the differences between these perceptions and to deal with the problems of living, people manipulate their environment and thus create new strategies for managing their lives. This type of adaptive behavior has occurred among the deaf.

The major factors that have together created special adaptations among the aged deaf are language, the peer group, geographic location, occupation, voluntary associations, and transportation. These factors are not of themselves innovative. Some of them represent typical patterns of American culture. It is the manipulation of these various aspects of culture that has had such a dramatic effect on the deaf. Meanwhile, personal development and community formation have interacted to create an environment that varies from the dominant pattern of American life in old age. The progression of events leading to behavior that is adaptive for old age is summarized below.

1. The Role of Language

In early childhood some alienation from the family of origin usually occurred unless the parents were deaf. Social and emotional distance arose out of the difficulties that surrounded parent-child communication and language learning, a factor that has profoundly affected the course of life.

As in any other culture, language has played a crucial role in the way in which the culture has evolved. The creation of a speech community based on sign language is probably the single most significant factor in the formation and maintenance of the deaf community. Sign language has had a dramatic influence on group development. By providing linguistic boundaries it has effectively segregated the deaf from the rest of society. Part of this segregation has arisen from the stigma attached to the language. Had the use of the language not been surrounded by such negative sanctions, it is unlikely that the separation of the aged deaf from the rest of society would be as pronounced as it is.[1]

2. The Emergence of a Peer-based Society

In middle childhood the family of origin was replaced by the peer group as the primary agent of socialization. Consequently, the peer group has unique meaning for the deaf individual. The clustering of deaf children in special schools *before* they developed language made family ties more complex. At the same time, the scarcity of adults with whom to interact caused children to depend on each other. The peer group was fostered in this way.

3. The Importance of Deaf Identity

By the time individuals reached adulthood, deafness had become the principal component of identity. The normalization process developed to offset the social stigma of deafness in the larger society. Deaf identity has continued to strengthen with time, through continual reinforcement from personal experience and from one's social interactions. In old age the individual's identity as a deaf person directs thought and action

---

1. If the current trend of increased awareness and acceptance of sign language continues, it is likely that future generations of deaf people will experience considerably less segregation from society than did the elderly deaf. When sign language is used and recognized by a sizable proportion of people, it becomes a normative mode of communication, and deaf people have more integral roles in their communities. Nora Groce's (1978) sociolinguistic study of the use of sign language in pre-twentieth-century Martha's Vineyard, where the incidence of deafness was 1 in 25, demonstrates this shift in attitude and behavior.

and dictates statuses and roles. It provides a sense of connectedness and fends off feelings of worthlessness, alienation, and isolation.

4. The Effect of Living Patterns

Certain patterns in daily-living situations developed as individuals left school and began to make their way in the world. During the early twentieth century the United States was changing from a rural to an urban society. Coincidentally, the occupations taught in special schools were skills most appropriate to the urban environment. Trades, such as those in the building and printing industries, have the greatest demand in the cities. The difficulties experienced by deaf people in getting jobs resulted in people settling where the demand was greatest.

The deaf person working in industry away from the deaf school tended not to develop friendships with co-workers because of the communication barrier. This factor detracted from job satisfaction and emphasized in-group sociability.

Marriage within the deaf community led to a language-based society of deaf couples who established their families in urban areas. Deaf people moved to the edges of the cities or into suburbs where they could live less expensively than in central city areas. They also tended to move near other deaf people. Thus, within the urban area a spatial pattern developed of dispersed clumps of families. The same type of spatial dispersal has been noted by Ablon (1971) in her study of Samoan-Americans. Among the deaf, however, the lack of telephones led to a restructuring of social activity.

5. The Development of Interdependency

The age-integrated deaf community fostered close interdependency. In old age deaf people are settled in urban areas to a disproportionate degree, rounding out a lifelong pattern of urban settlement. They seek each other out to avoid social isolation. In *The Heart Is a Lonely Hunter*, a novel in which the main character is the only deaf person in a small town, Carson Mc-Cullers (1940) captures the meaning and extent of such complete isolation.

As deaf people became urban dwellers they developed patterns to cope with the dispersed social environment. Life in the city without a telephone presents a number of problems, large and small, such as how to avoid isolation, maximize safety, and maintain contact with friends. As cars became an important part of American life they also became a part of life in the deaf community and led, eventually, to the expression "My car is my phone."

Voluntary associations and the national network of deaf people played important roles in this community. To facilitate social interaction, deaf people set up special meeting places and established deaf clubs in the big cities. Having central meeting places is a social institution that has endured through the years. As was noted earlier, deaf people join voluntary associations throughout adult life.

Voluntary associations continue to be a vital socializing force in old age. To meet their needs, the deaf elderly began to use resources offered to the general population of old people; senior citizen groups provided anticipatory socialization and strengthened the mutual support system.

6. The Reemergence of the Peer Group

In old age compensatory reemergence of the peer group occurs as relationships with hearing children and grandchildren attenuate. Considerable intergenerational interaction continues because of the small size of the deaf community. The usual criteria of personal preference operate in cliques and subgroupings (e.g., ethnicity, religion), but proximity begins to play a more important role as mobility declines with advancing age.

While the peer group continues to be important during adult life, perhaps more so than in the rest of society, it is in old age that there is a resurgence of the extremely strong support that membership in this group affords. Involvement in peer-group relationships in old age provides an arena in which reciprocity and interdependence can be maintained.

7. The Significance of Adaptive Strategies for Old Age

Stigma and exclusion based on the disability continue to affect the deaf in old age, in some instances intensified by negative attitudes toward the aged. But in spite of this, the status of these aged deaf people is not a miserable one. Strategies for coping with disability and marginality are already well learned. Therefore, the self-images of those in the study sample do not suffer markedly in old age.

TEMPORAL DYNAMICS

Adaptive behavior is not only innovative, it is dynamic. Adaptation occurs over time on both an individual and a cultural level. Over the life-span there is an interplay between individual life histories and the historical development of the community.

THE DEVELOPMENT OF COPING SKILLS

When I began my research I hypothesized that, although the disability retards development early in life, by old age the individual has caught up with his or her hearing contemporaries in social functioning. Delayed development is an important factor in the adaptive behavior of the deaf, one that has significance in old age. As a result of delayed development, the individual spends most of his or her life trying to catch up with American society. "Catching up" occurs over the life course, and is probably completed in middle age.

We do know that old deaf people have developed a repertoire of coping behavior that most of them lacked in early adulthood. In old age deaf people acknowledge changes that have occurred in their behavior over the life-span. Community leaders, when speaking to the elderly deaf about the problems of deaf youth, invariably point out the contrast in coping ability between young and old, and acknowledge the success the old have had in making life adjustments.

Personal development itself is affected by culture, and delayed development has repercussions across the life-span. It is apparent that there is considerably more variation than stage theorists have described (Erikson, 1950). For the deaf delayed development is an important factor in the cultural fit that occurs in old age.

The repertoire of coping behavior in late life is the result of lifelong socialization and the resolution of identity conflicts. The efforts of the aged deaf to achieve mastery over the environment, an American value (Kalish, 1975:85), have been relatively successful.

SOCIALIZATION

Socialization to American society is an ongoing process for everyone, although we seldom refer to it in this way. The changing nature of culture requires people to keep in step. Just as the individual who spends time in prison must be resocialized afterward, socialization is especially important for a subsociety such as that in which the deaf live. Socialization never ceases, and in fact may be heightened in old age if people have increased access to the outside world. Deaf people must actively work to keep abreast of trends in the hearing world because they cannot monitor both worlds as can a bilingual ethnic group member who can hear.

As was mentioned in earlier chapters, one purpose of sociability is to exchange information of both a personal and an impersonal nature. We all do this as a matter of course. Deaf people, however, underline the importance of information exchange out of a sense of urgent necessity. They do not limit themselves to information; thoughts, feelings, reactions, and opinions are all a part of the learning process. Interchanges are complex, not simply informational. Over time, these exchanges become increasingly intimate. Because the deaf individual is limited to the deaf community for meaningful communication, intense relationships develop and are carried on over the life cycle *with the same people.* These life-term relationships allow the person freedom of self-expression, provide continuity, and ultimately make personal growth possible. At the same time, however, the limited nature of relationships in the bounded community creates group dynamics that are parochial and thus similar to those of a peasant village. The limited social world affects personality and world view and ultimately shapes the direction adaptive strategies take.

Old deaf people have used their social circles over the lifespan to reconcile many problems of living, to learn the ways of the hearing world, to do "identity work," and to normalize. In old age the problems of youth are behind them, but the structure to deal with those problems is still there.

THE LIFE REVIEW

One of the primary tasks of the social group in old age is to provide an atmosphere conducive to life review (Butler, 1963). He conceptualized the life review as "a naturally-occurring, universal mental process characterized by the progressive return to consciousness of past experiences and particularly, the resurgence of unresolved conflicts. . . . These revived experiences can be surveyed and reintegrated" (p. 66). The aged deaf have a sign summarizing this process that means "looking backward."

Erikson (1950:268–269) in his model of life stages refers to the last stage of life as ego integrity. The parameters of ego integrity include a basic acceptance of one's life as inevitable, appropriate, and meaningful, while overcoming the fear of death. Gerontologists perceive this final effort at personal resolution as an important component in rounding out the lifespan.

When individuals go through life as members of an age-graded group, as do the deaf, they will experience life transitions together. In old age these relationships are especially important in the individual's adaptation to aging. A high level of peer interaction facilitates socialization to aging, the development of an aging identity, and increased opportunities to articulate the life review. These processes, taken together, allow the deaf person to integrate old age into personal identity.

THE SYMBOLIC NATURE OF COMMUNITY

As we have seen, language, communal institutions, and boundaries all play a role in the development and maintenance of community. Most important of all, however, are the symbolic ties between the individual and the group, those *felt* bonds that the individual has for members of the group. This experiential/feeling aspect of community has been called "communitas" (Turner, 1969:96). To the aged deaf the peer group symbolizes communitas and, even more, injects every other part of life with meaning. The peer group offers assurance that the individual will be able to express himself or herself in language. For the deaf the need for self-expression through language is so great that all of the accouterments of self-expression have become emotionally charged, particularly the peer group, which symbolizes this self-expression. In consequence, a great deal of the interaction that takes place in the peer group has ritual significance, which reinforces the symbolic bonds that tie individuals to one another.

The group lives in a continual state of threatened extinction from the outside world. They are subject to threats from outside forces for a variety of reasons. In order to cope with these threats, they must continually reinforce the symbols of their collective identity.

Language evolves in vertical progressions through time. Sign language, however, unlike other languages, is passed horizontally rather than vertically (Meadow, 1974:5) because there are few kinship ties between the generations. The deaf children of deaf parents are the linguistic links between generations. These individuals provide a sense of continuity to the language and to the culture itself. The culture is passed on from one generation to the next, however, not only because of these individuals, but because the generations are linguistically mutually intelligible and share a collective identity.

The language is extremely vulnerable to change and upheaval. Change comes not only from within, that is, through the natural changes that take place in any language over time, but from outside as well. Historically, the oral approach to deaf education posed a threat to sign language. Today these threats are in the form of new sign-language systems based on English, which are now being taught to increasing numbers of deaf children and are much less severe in magnitude.

Significantly, the culture is carried on by the peer group rather than by an enduring institution such as the family. Group members must consequently work overtime to sustain and promote the group, because it exists in an uneasy truce with kin ties. Allegiance divided between kin and nonkin is a source of stress in deaf society.

Despite the "cultural frailty" of the deaf community—for example, the paucity of such common institutional supports as kin and ethnicity—it has continuity across the generations. The aged deaf share a collective identity with all other deaf people. Their collective identity is based on a status devalued by disability. They have legitimized their status in their own eyes through the normalization process.

Another force at work is the threat of extinction by decimation of the group's numbers. Like a small band of hunters and gatherers, the deaf need to maintain a balance with their environment. They are concerned with their social survival and, consequently, must exert social pressure on all members to participate in group interaction.

In old age the group is thwarted by deaths in its membership. Life as they know it is ending. They fear that deaf youth of the future may not even have mutually intelligible language, much less the same value system. These concerns are assuaged by the knowledge that deafness continues to be a medical problem for which there are no medical solutions. This factor, together with the increased acceptance and use of sign language, whatever its form, gives the group a sense of continuity.

Aged deaf people share feelings of pride that they have worked, raised families, and dealt with the problems of life as well as with their disability. The shared sense of accomplishment allows them to collectively resolve questions related to generativity, a term coined by Erikson (1950) to refer to productivity and creativity, especially as they relate to establishing and guiding the next generation.

There appears to be a relationship between the size of the social group and the values to which it subscribes. The values of American culture emphasize independence, individualism, and competition, and as Clark and Anderson (1967:425) point out, these values must be acted out through work and a whirl of social activity if the individual is to avoid the label "useless" in old age. In contrast, the values of small societies emphasize interdependence, mutuality, and cooperation, qualities that are more advantageous for the aging process (Cowgill and Holmes, 1972:12). These latter values are most often observable in small societies where relationships with others are based on face-to-face contact. Although the value systems of complex societies cannot be restructured to meet the needs of the elderly, the stress of the value conflicts created by cultural dissonance could be diminished by the increased participation of the individual in small communities within the complex society. It has been demonstrated that the cohesive community is a positive force in urban life for all age groups (Stein, 1960; Gans, 1962) and for the elderly in particular (Rosow, 1967).

The aged have little to offer that is valued by other Americans. The breakdown of reciprocity between young and old causes strain on the society, particularly on the elderly (Clark, 1967). In contrast, the elderly deaf play a vital role in their community. The old have a vested interest in the young and in passing on their culture to younger deaf people. In turn, younger deaf people value the elderly for their historic meaning to the community and for their financial support of deaf organizations. Ongoing reciprocal relationships provide old people with a sense of continuity, while the collective identity gives meaning to their lives.

XI

Aging in American Life: Implications of Studying the Aged Deaf

The way that deaf people live out the final stage of life raises questions about other old people in relation to the themes that have emerged in this study. Now that we have traced the lives of these disabled people and the way they cope with their disability, certain similarities become apparent between the lifelong devalued status of deaf people and the status of most Americans in old age. This observation leads us to ask how old age itself is like disability, and what its repercussions are on the individual.

Another theme of this study has been the part that age peers play for the deaf throughout life, especially in old age. The crucial role of age peers in adaptation brings us to the question of their role among other age-graded groups of elderly people.

A third consideration has been the membership older deaf people have in their community, its import for their collective identity, and their similarity to a minority group. This theme raises the question of what ethnic minority group membership means for other elderly people, and its influence on their lives.

Finally, the overall adaptive behavior of the deaf in old age was noted, and the importance of some of these factors in adaptation to late life. To take this concern one step further, we need to ask whether such adaptive strategies represent successful aging, and what is the role younger members of society play in this process. As Americans live into prolonged old age, there is increasing concern with negotiating this last stage of life with meaning and dignity. In this last chapter we shall look at some of the personal and social aspects of behavior that constitute adaptation in old age. Thus, this chapter is really an epilogue, in which the implications of the findings for other aged Americans will be examined.

OLD AGE AS DISABILITY

The disabled represent a relatively small proportion of the population in any society. Response to disability varies cross-culturally (Sigerist, 1943), as does the status of disabled people (Hanks and Hanks, 1948). Magical powers are attributed to the disabled in some societies, and a special status is developed for them, while in other societies the disabled are viewed as the embodiment of evil and are killed or abandoned. The criteria for determining disability are usually social rather than physical and are based on the individual's ability to function within the group (Watson and Maxwell, 1977).

In complex societies the status of the disabled is a devalued one regardless of the individual's level of functioning. In their discussion of the sick role in American society, Parsons and Fox (1958) state that failure to return to one's previous state of functioning after a certain period of time has elapsed constitutes a form of deviance, and that others will begin to perceive the individual as deviant. Sick-role theory has led to a considerable literature on the role of illness in social functioning. When permanent physical disability occurs, however, the parameters of the sick role are no longer applicable. As individuals and their families adapt to permanent role changes, the sick role loses its relevance (Kassebaum and Baumann, 1965). Thus, sick-role theory has limited application within American society; it nevertheless reflects our cultural biases about individuals who do not carry "their share" in society. The individual's status in society is undermined by disability. The disabled individual is continually trying to adapt to a society that makes few exceptions for physical differences.

Old age is like disability to the extent that being old affects one's roles and statuses and invokes an ascribed status similar in its effect to that experienced by the disabled. The status of old people cross-culturally has been a matter for debate since Leo Simmons (1945) theorized that the aged in tribal and peasant societies maintain more status than they do in complex societies. In contrast, Lipman (1970) states that the aged have never been held in high regard universally, while Arth (1972) suggests that the aged do not necessarily receive veneration in tribal society and cites the Ibo as an example. The theory that as modernization increases the status of the aged in society tends to decrease (Cowgill and Holmes, 1972) has been tested by Bengston et al. (1975). Their findings confirm this theory on a societal level, but not on an individual level. They suggest that individual responses to aging may not be directly reflected in societal attitudes, and that individual and societal attitudes toward aging should be considered separately from each other.

One component of status of the aged is the nature of deference paid to them. The degree to which younger people defer to their elders reflects the status of the aged in a given culture—for example, the considerable deference paid to elders in traditional Chinese society. In his study of prestige of the aged in Portugal, Lipman (1970) found that behavior of younger people toward the aged was based on two factors: (1) ritual deference and (2) realistic appraisal. Maxwell and Silverman (1978), in their study of deference in ninety-five societies, found that deference behavior can be broken down into three categories: (1) victual or "custodial," (2) ceremonial, and (3) linguistic. It would appear that the *quality* of deference is highly related to whether or not the aged individual has a viable role in the society in which he or she lives. In cultures where old people participate in a meaningful way, they continue to be an integral part of their society. In tribal and peasant societies the acknowledgment of past function is often sufficient to keep the old person integrated into society. For example, O'Nell (1972) found that continued responsibility among the Zapotec in old age contributed to ongoing participation in the society, and that even when the individual had relinquished all responsibility, the fact of past responsibility contributed to continuing respect and deference. He notes, however, that the fewer ongoing responsibilities the aged person had, the more likely the deference shown him or her was ritualistic.

In complex society the status of the elderly is much more vulnerable. It has been defined as an ascribed status akin to that of a terminal sick role (Lipman and Sterne, 1969). Arluke and Peterson (1977:10) state that as a result of assignment to the sick role old age has come to be defined as an unnatural state, and the process of aging itself a pathology.

In societies such as that of the United States, where the power is largely in the hands of younger people, old age is deprecated on a societal level, although the quality of individual experience varies greatly. The old person in the United States is the focus of certain cultural attitudes about growing old. Negative attitudes about aging have become a cultural norm. The national concern with aging is not merely with old age—for example, what to do after retirement—but with the actual passage of time and its meaning to the individual. The widespread popularity of books such as *Passages* (Sheehy, 1976), which deal with the ongoing trauma that aging has become, underlines our vulnerability to this inevitable process.

These negative attitudes about aging have resulted in old age becoming a devalued status and have led to theories that attempt to draw parallels between old age and other devalued statuses.

OLD AGE AND MINORITY-GROUP CHARACTERISTICS

The attributes of old age that resemble disability are the same ones that have led to the characterization of the aged as a minority group. As was mentioned in chapter two, the deaf are one group of disabled people who have been defined as a minority group (Vernon and Makowsky, 1969), and they see themselves in this way. Similarly, arguments have been advanced that the aged constitute a minority group (Barron, 1953). Certain minority-group characteristics, such as devalued status, do apply to the aged; however, the aged cannot be characterized in this way, because they lack homogeneity and a common identity (Streib, 1965). The minority-group concept has arisen because the aged, together with ethnic and disabled minorities, are disenfranchised in the United States.

The concept of double jeopardy refers to people who are members of ethnic minorities and are old as well; it hypothesizes that individuals who hold such dual status (for example, people who are both black and old) will be at higher risk than the general population of old people (Jackson, 1971). Research based on the double-jeopardy hypothesis with aged whites, blacks, and Mexican-Americans found that minority-group members are at a greater risk with regard to some variables, such as health and income; on the other hand, they found that minority-group membership did not have an adverse effect on patterns of social interaction and life satisfaction (Dowd and Bengston, 1978).

THE EFFECT OF DEVALUED STATUS

Many Americans experience a devalued status for the first time when they become old. Glaser and Strauss (1971) describe the process of undergoing such a transition as a "status passage." The new status involves significant changes in one's sense of self. Feelings of resentment, self-hatred, and depression are common responses to negative changes in status in old age (Clark and Anderson, 1967).

Social scientists who have written about disability have examined the problem of devalued status at length (e.g., Wright, 1960; Goffman, 1963; McDaniel, 1969), as have social scientists studying aging (Clark and Anderson, 1967; Rosow, 1973; Neugarten and Hagestad, 1977). Regardless of the context, devalued status has a negative influence on the individual's sense of self, coping mechanisms, social relationships, and overall functioning (Goffman, 1963; Clark and Anderson, 1967). The term *devalued status* encompasses two actual kinds of status: (1) continuing low-value status—for example, the lifelong process experienced by the deaf—and (2) loss of status, the status passage experienced by most people as they become old. This difference influences the way people cope with status loss in old age.

When low status occurs early in life, as with the aged deaf, the individual has a far better chance of learning to cope with it over a lifetime than does the individual who acquires such a status late in life. It is likely that coping with the stigma attached to low status early in life helps one to cope with old age, particularly if the previous status is more stigmatizing than that of old age. Jackson, Bacon, and Peterson (1977–78) reached the same conclusions regarding aged blacks, and suggested that "adjustment to aging, particularly psychologically, might be a different and perhaps relatively easier task in comparison to the adjustment of white majority individuals" (p. 177).

The techniques for dealing with devalued status in old age are similar to those for dealing with a disability. As was noted for the deaf, these techniques range from realism to denial. Bultena and Powers (1978) state that the reason there is so much denial of aging in American society is the degrading nature of the old person's status. Old age is the first stage of life with systematic status loss for an entire cohort (Rosow, 1973).

We can make some inferences about devalued status based on symbolic interaction theory, the concept that individuals perceive themselves in relation to how they think the world perceives them (George Herbert Mead, 1934). Those people with whom the individual interacts, and the attitudes those others hold in relation to the individual, have a profound effect on the old person's sense of self. From a study of identity among white, middle-class elderly people in a metropolitan area, Kaufman (1980) concluded that age is not a major component of the self-concept or of a person's self-image, and that people do not relate who they are to time. Rather, the experiences of one's whole life contribute to self-image. It is likely that in old age the cumulative effect on self-image deflects feelings of devaluation to some extent and prevents total social paralysis from taking place.

The effects of devalued status are nevertheless profound. In a study of over three hundred people sixty years of age and older, Ward (1977:232) found that there was a strong relationship between acceptance of negative attitudes toward old people and self-derogation and suggests that stigmatization has a significant impact on the well-being of older people. The degree to which stigmatization is felt and personalized by the old person is undoubtedly related to perceived stigma by significant others—family, close friends, and peers. Hyman (1971) suggests that perception of stigma is related to familial attitudes among older individuals recovering from stroke; in his study, those who perceived themselves as stigmatized did less well in rehabilitation than those who did not perceive themselves in this way.

AGE-SEGREGATED COMMUNITIES

In recent years a trend has emerged in complex society: the development of age-segregated communities of the old. Such communities are not dispersed, as is the deaf community, but are oriented around a physical environment in which people live in close proximity to each other. They are representative of the increasing tendency toward age-graded environments. Community studies of this sort include public housing (Rosow, 1967; Hochschild, 1973; Ross, 1977; Goist, 1978), mobile home parks (Sheila Johnson, 1971; Angrosino, 1976); and retirement communities where individuals purchase their own property (Bultena and Wood, 1969; Byrne, 1974; Jerry Jacobs, 1974; Fry, 1977).

Despite the fact that a very small proportion of the aged live in age-segregated or retirement housing (Neugarten and Hagestad, 1977), such living situations create considerable interest among gerontologists because of their potential influence on the development of social policy. Fry (1977) refers to these communities as "laboratories," and sees their primary value as providing cultural insights into urban society.

Age-grading is seen as the underlying reason for the success of retirement communities (Fry, 1977). Studies of age-segregated housing have demonstrated increased social interaction (Seguin, 1973). In his study of elderly people living in old apartment buildings, Rosow (1967) found that those individuals who lived in buildings where 40 or 50 percent of the tenants were elderly benefited from the socialization that took place as a result of living among so many age peers. Rosow (1974) postulates that increased social interaction with age peers provides anticipatory socialization to old age.

Studies of morale have also been done in age-segregated housing (Sherman, 1975; Bultena, 1974), but the relationship between morale and residence is not as clear as it is for social interaction. Bultena and Powers (1978:753) found that comparisons with age peers are important to the formulation of age-identities, a process that usually takes place in age-segregated settings. Ross (1977) points out, "The general relationship between separate residence and morale reflects other consequences of living with people the same age: emergence of norms, definitions of older neighbors as role models and reference groups, development of an age identity, and potential help in emergencies" (p. 177).

Identification with a reference group of peers can be based on ethnicity, on language, or on a particular set of shared experiences that the group holds in common. Ross (1977:5) has referred to this sense of shared identity as "we-feeling." Of the various components of community, we-feeling is probably the strongest underlying element in community formation. Individuals in these communities share certain features at the time they enter, such as homogeneous backgrounds, investment, and exclusive social ties (Ross, 1977:178–182).

Do these processes necessarily occur in all age-segregated environments? Apparently, much depends on the degree of control individuals exert over their environment. Kleemeier (1954) suggested that institutions that have social control over older people will negatively affect social participation. Goist (1979) compared a public housing project in Leeds, England, with one in Cleveland, Ohio. She found that individuals in the Leeds project developed a sense of group identity, while those in the Cleveland project did not. She attributes this difference to the control the Leeds individuals had over their environment; they played an important role in decision-making in their housing project. In contrast, residents of the Cleveland project were not included in the decision-making process. These findings are similar to Angrosino's (1976). He found that "community" did not develop in a Florida mobile home park he studied, because residents did not participate in decision-making.

Rosow's (1967) findings on the importance of age-graded environments for ongoing socialization coincided with early evidence of satisfactory age-segregated housing; this factor may have influenced the development of the idea that total age-segregation in housing is ideal for people (Carp, 1977: 285). Teaff et al. (1978) have since carried out a study of public housing for the aged, carefully controlled for age-segregation. Their findings support the hypothesis that frequent contact with age peers is supportive. They limit their conclusions to public housing, since they did not include private housing as a control in their study.

Age segregation reflects on a grand scale the same dilemma that the aged deaf face. The benefits of life in an age-graded setting are many—for example, the extension of social network, the development of age consciousness, and the creation of group-specific norms and roles. It is probable that the age-segregated environment helps people cope with their devalued status in society. Life in a planned environment "buffers" the individual from societal attitudes because the individual relates predominantly to age peers. Membership in such a reference group reduces the effect of negative perceptions by blunting one's awareness of stigma. Identification with the group thus affects the consequences of devaluation, as it does for deaf people.

On the other hand, these positive factors may be undermined by feelings of marginality if the planned environment does not meet all of the individual's social needs. For it is only within the group that the individual receives validation of self and is immune to the stigma attached to advancing age. Interactions outside of the group, especially with significant others, may heighten awareness of stigma and consequently undermine morale. Seguin (1973) says that individuals have a choice: they can live in the wider community and experience the social and personal isolation associated with role loss or they can live in the isolated retirement community, "but with the provision of personal mental health, social functioning, and role adequacy within the contained peer population" (p. 214).

To further complicate the question of age-segregation, it must be noted that age-segregation is similar to that of racial segregation in that it breeds stereotypes. Lofland (1968) states that lack of face-to-face interaction between members of different age groups is conducive to the formation and maintenance of age stereotypes. Increased age-segregation has already contributed to the development of stereotypes about old people in the United States. Ward's (1977) study, cited earlier, demonstrates that older people not only are aware of age stereotypes but internalize them and consequently suffer from their stigmatizing effects. This process would naturally affect the attitudes of older people toward younger people and facilitate the creation of stereotypes about the young. We can only speculate about how the continuance of this trend will affect intergenerational relationships in the future.

The study of age-segregated communities demonstrates that, under the right conditions, people can establish viable communities in old age without having known each other all their lives. In old age these communities are powerful tools in keeping people actively involved with each other and with the world around them.

ETHNIC COMMUNITIES

The great number of old people in the United States tends to obscure the question of scale in gerontological research. The fact that millions of aged Americans identify themselves with an ethnic group or with a special community is generally touched on only tangentially, if at all, as testimony to community cohesiveness or the lack of it. Ethnic communities are usually studied without emphasis on age, unless the study focuses on the process of acculturation across the generations.

Two perspectives in studying the role of the aged in ethnic communities are (1) ethnic identity and (2) exchange theory.

ETHNIC IDENTITY

We have seen the important roles that identity and group membership play in the lives of the aged deaf. Ascribed membership in an ethnic community is very similar to membership in the deaf community in that it automatically provides the individual with a reference group, for which most individuals develop a sense of identification. The degree to which people continue to identify and maintain ties with the ethnic group are intensified as their dwindling social roles force them to fall back on their ascribed statuses.

Those ethnic groups that are most Americanized will probably attribute the most devalued status to old age. Cuellar (1978) found that Mexican-Americans tend to experience devalued status in old age, and he attributes this finding to the acceptance of mainstream American attitudes about aging. The impact of devalued status was reduced for those Mexican-Americans who joined voluntary associations; they constructed social arenas of peers and acquired a sense of personal worth from participation in these groups (Cuellar, 1978:229). Thus, maintenance or renewal of an ethnic or quasi-ethnic membership is particularly important in old age when social roles are diminished. Kiefer (1974) says of Japanese-Americans: ". . . being part of a minority itself might have some large benefits for the aged. . . . They are a little community unto themselves, tightly bound by the sharing of a unique identity" (p. 238).

In ethnic enclaves in the United States, the family continues to be a primary vehicle through which ethnic identity is maintained and bolstered over a lifetime. Lithuanians maintain ethnic identity through group and family ties; the three-generation household is commonplace (Baškauskas, 1977:151). In her study of impoverished black families, Stack (1974) found that three-generation households play a crucial role in creating bonds and establishing lifelong networks. Braroe (1975), in a discussion of mobility patterns of young Crees, comments that grandparents take care of their grandchildren for extended periods of time while the parents are moving about, and that frequently these household patterns of grandparents and grandchildren become permanent ones. The continuation of such extended-family living situations ensures that older people maintain integral roles in the family and play an important part in transmitting cultural knowledge to their grandchildren. In this process ethnic identity is being maintained, and a form of social exchange is taking place as well.

SOCIAL EXCHANGE

Within some ethnic and subcultural enclaves in complex society the aged keep their status through various types of social exchange, and in the process they maintain viable roles in these groups. For example, Jackson (1976) has described the importance of grandparenting to the functioning of the black extended family, while Colleen Johnson (1979) has discussed godparenting, or *comparaggio*, in terms of its importance in sociability and exchange among Italian-Americans.

The argument, advanced by Dowd (1975) and based on exchange theory, that the aged must have some negotiable commodity to exchange in order to maintain their status in society is especially true in complex societies. Unless the aged have something of worth desired by younger people, their status will be devalued. As Maxwell and Silverman (1970) have pointed out, the aged have traditionally been an important source of information in society, a factor that directly relates to their participation and esteem in the community. With the advent of rapid technological change and its resulting effect on the dissemination of information, that function is greatly diminished. However, when aged persons continue to be involved in the exchange of services, their status is not greatly impaired.

Whenever an ethnic group wishes to preserve its cultural identity, the old person's worth in the community goes up. In such situations, identity can be viewed both as a commodity and as a personal affirmation of self. This perspective is based on the assumption of congruence between exchange theory and symbolic interaction theory (Singlemann, 1972). That is, identity becomes a desired commodity that is subject to exchange in much the same way as other services. In her study of aged Corsicans in Paris, Cool (1979) found that ethnicity became an adaptive strategy that provided old people with social identity, the potential for ongoing social relationships, and a source of power in their relations with younger people in the community. There are considerable similarities between this ethnic group and the aged deaf. The deaf have formed a small, homogeneous group in the urban area, and their adaptive strategies have followed similar patterns.

The recent surge of interest in the United States in finding and maintaining one's "roots" is reflected in recent findings on generations and ethnic identity. Clark, Kaufman, and Pierce (1976) found two types of responses among third-generation Japanese- and Mexican-Americans toward their ethnic background. Regardless of the ethnicity of respondents, some appeared to be highly anglicized, while others identified strongly with their ethnic background and frequently idealized the culture of origin, even when they had limited knowledge about it. Thus, the degree to which younger generations are anglicized has an effect on the status of the aged and their ability to use their identity as a means of social exchange. In Cuellar's (1978) study of Mexican-Americans cited earlier, where acceptance of majority attitudes about aging took place, identity was an important component in solidifying the peer group, but did not appear to play an important part in intergenerational relations. In contrast, Williams (1979), in a study of aged Indians in Oklahoma, found that the "Indianness" of the aged, and their knowledge of cultural traditions, were so highly valued by younger Indians as to create a source of strain between young and old. The old could not recall all the historical details of past ways of life, and as a result they fell short of younger people's expectations.

We can draw some conclusions about ethnicity in relation to aging from the preceding discussion. First of all, it appears that ethnicity is a more intrinsic part of one's identity than aging is, and provides a greater potential for high self-valuation. The degree to which ethnicity cushions the individual from the attitudes of the dominant society depends on one's world view. If the individual embraces the ethnic group to the exclusion of the outside world, his or her self-concept will be shaped primarily by the attitudes of the ethnic group. The degree to which the individual is concerned with the attitudes and regard of the larger society will have an influence on the individual's self-concept and the way in which it incorporates age.

Second, the degree to which younger generations adhere to the values and beliefs about aging that are held by the dominant society will influence the well-being of older individuals. Apparently, in those groups where ethnic traditions are venerated, the aged are most likely to retain meaningful roles in their community. Cool (1978) states that "to revere one's old relatives and to listen to their teachings are ways to indicate one's being Niolan [Corsican]. . . . The old always represent proximity to that mythical time of ethnic purity before the contamination by the larger society and its values" (pp. 9–10).

Thus, if the individual has a strong sense of identification with the group, which is shared by younger generations, and if, at the same time, attitudes about aging differ from those of the dominant society, the aged will probably not experience the degree of devaluation experienced by most aged Americans. In such groups functional roles for the aged will enhance feelings of self-worth and decrease the effect of devaluation.

SUCCESSFUL AGING

Now that we have examined some of the variations in patterns of aging and some of the problems people experience as they grow old, the question arises, What leads to successful aging? Obviously, factors relating to the self as well as to the individual's interaction with the social system are involved in the process of adaptation to old age. Maintaining one's social and emotional equilibrium is not easy in the face of the cultural contradictions that surround aging in American society. Certain elements appear to be crucial in an individual's life if he or she is to negotiate the final stage of life successfully. These elements share the overall theme of continuity, made especially vital by the cultural discontinuities of old age.

On the personal level, a sense of self-consistency is extremely important in old age. Neugarten (1972) states that persons age in ways that are consistent with their previous life histories. The subjective experience of aging may be quite different from that perceived by others, however. Whether or not a person experiences feelings of consistency in his or her life undoubtedly influences well-being. This sense of consistency is quite independent of the actual realities of change, both in the individual and in the surrounding world. The sense of consistency is the thread that runs through people's lives and anchors them. As Kiefer (1974:232) says, "a large part of the problem of adaptation is maintaining the illusion of consistency amid the facts of change."

Related to the need for consistency is the need for flexibility. In citing the adaptive tasks of aging, Clark and Anderson (1967) emphasize the need for awareness and acceptance of changes in oneself, as well as the need to come to terms with society's perception of the aged. Huyck (1974) states that the ability to make choices and to appreciate the experiences available at every stage of life is important to the aging process. In other words, the ability to be self-actualizing is important in adapting to old age. In order to be self-actualizing, however, old people must work within the confines that society, and age itself, places on them. As Clark and Anderson (1967) suggest, aging individuals must modify their values to reflect the realities of their age. For example, independence, so fiercely cherished in American life by young and old alike, must be translated into interdependence in old age in order to be adaptive. Perhaps one reason retirement communities have been so successful is that it is easier to establish interdependence with peers than it is with younger people. Generally speaking, interdependence is more common between peers in American life than it is across generations.

Unless the aged hold some power in their community, relationships with younger people tend to become skewed, and dependency for the old results. Thus, in groups that share a strong sense of identity, interdependence is usually maintained because aged individuals have viable roles that keep them integrated into the group.

Generativity, mentioned earlier in regard to the aged deaf, is of the utmost importance in maintaining one's sense of continuity. Individuals have a need to put themselves in the context of a greater time perspective than their own life encompasses. This is especially true in late life when society's negative messages about old age contradict lifelong values about the worth of an individual's existence. Myerhoff (1978b: 164) states that continuity is essential for psychological well-being and personal integration, and cites four kinds of continuity: social, cultural, personal life-historical, and spiritual. The ways that continuity manifests itself for the individual vary, but probably the most typical is the experience of Japanese-Americans cited by Kiefer (1974). In his study of three generations of Japanese-Americans, Kiefer notes that the aged gain considerable fulfillment from observing their children and grandchildren carry out the traditions the aged began in the United States.

The maintenance of one's social equilibrium in society is intertwined with the personal sense of continuity. Although much of this chapter has been devoted to a discussion of the disadvantages of old age, I have also tried to show that the aging individual has resources that can be used to his or her advantage. These resources include cultural commodities that can be exchanged within one's society or social group. Lozier and Althouse (1974), in their study of an Appalachian community, found that status within the community, exemplified by property and "standing," was an important commodity for exchange with younger people. We have seen how the aged deaf exchange the same commodities and consequently exert an element of control over community decision-making. When older people play such a part in community life, they are less likely to suffer from the effects of role loss and the consequent changes it imposes on self-image.

The ability to exchange cultural commodities brings power and the ability to manipulate the environment, conditions that are the antithesis of stereotypes of old age. Power takes many forms and can be expressed in a variety of ways (Simic, 1978:18). When the aged have a modicum of power in their community, they are in a position to upgrade their collective status. Lozier and Althouse (1974) state that "conduct leading to successful aging involves the construction of a protective social environment, through the obligating of juniors, within a social system that can be counted on to enforce the obligations" (p. 80).

It is this last point that brings us back to the question of old age as disability. When the social system no longer enforces obligations to elders, or indeed even recognizes obligations, disequilibrium is established, thus reducing the aging individual's position in the social system to a marginal one similar to that of the disabled. In order to maintain a toehold in the social system, the individual must negotiate a position in society for himself or herself, using all the resources at his or her disposal. Whether this position is in an age-graded community, in an ethnic group, or in a social network made up of family and friends is irrelevant. What is of crucial importance is that the individual exchange something of cultural significance, mutually valued by young and old, since cultural continuity is the framework on which all people build their lives.

Glossary

Adventitious hearing loss—Hearing loss that occurs before language is acquired

American Sign Language—A language of manual signs which differs grammatically and syntactically from English

Deafness—As used here, a severe to profound hearing loss, which interferes with the ability to hear in the speech frequencies

Expressive ability—Ability to express oneself to others

Gallaudet College—Liberal arts college for the deaf in Washington, D.C.

Hard of hearing—A moderate to severe hearing loss which interferes with, but does not prohibit, the ability to understand speech

Hearing—Often used as a noun, as in "a hearing who lived next door to me"

Hearing world—Everything outside of the deaf community

Lip-reading / speech-reading—Reading information on the lips of others

Manual method—Teaching method based on the use of sign language and the manual alphabet

Oral method—Teaching method based on lip-reading and the development of speech

Prelingual hearing loss—Hearing loss that occurs before language is acquired

Receptive ability—Ability to understand the communication of others

Total communication—Teaching method based on the combined use of manual and oral methods

Bibliography

Ablon, Joan
   1971   The Social Organization of an Urban Samoan Community.
      Southwestern Journal of Anthropology 27:75–96.
Angrosino, Michael V.
   1976   Anthropology and the Aged: A Preliminary Community
      Study. Gerontologist 16:174–180.
Arluke, Arnold, and John Peterson
   1977   Old Age as Illness: Notes on Accidental Medicalization. Pa-
      per presented at the Annual Meeting of the Society for Applied
      Anthropology, San Diego, Calif., April 6–9.
Arth, Malcolm
   1961   American Culture and the Phenomenon of Friendship in
      the Aged. Gerontologist 1(4):168–170.
   1972   Aging: A Cross-cultural Perspective. In Research Planning
      and Action for the Elderly. Donald P. Kent, Robert Kastenbaum,
      and Sylvia Sherwood, eds. Pp. 352–364. New York: Behavioral
      Publications.
Babchuk, Nicholas
   1965   Primary Friends and Kin: A Study of the Associations of
      Middle-Class Couples. Social Forces 43:483–493.
Banton, M., ed.
   1968   The Social Anthropology of Complex Societies. London:
      Tavistock Publications.
Barron, Milton L.
   1953   Minority Group Characteristics of the Aged in American
      Society. Journal of Gerontology 8:477–482.

Barth, Fredrik
  1969   Ethnic Groups and Boundaries. Boston: Little, Brown.
Baškauskas, Liucija
  1977   Multiple Identities: Adjusted Lithuanian Refugees in Los
         Angeles. Urban Anthropology 6:141–154.
Bell, Robert R.
  1971   Marriage and Family Interaction. Homewood, Ind.: Dorsey
         Press.
Bengston, Vern L., James J. Dowd, David H. Smith, and Alex Inkeles
  1975   Modernization, Modernity and Perceptions of Aging: A
         Cross-cultural Study. Journal of Gerontology 30:688–695.
Blenkner, M.
  1969   The Normal Dependencies of Aging. In Dependencies in
         Old Age. R. A. Kalish, ed. In Occasional Papers in Gerontology,
         Vol. 6. Ann Arbor and Detroit: Institute of Gerontology, Univer-
         sity of Michigan and Wayne State University.
Bott, Elizabeth
  1957   Family and Social Network. New York: Free Press.
Braroe, Neil
  1975   Indian and White: Self-Image and Interaction in a Canadian
         Plains Community. Stanford: Stanford University Press.
Brim, O., and S. Wheeler
  1966   Socialization after Childhood. New York: Wiley.
Brown, Roger W.
  1962   Language and Categories. In A Study of Thinking. J. S.
         Bruner, Jacqueline J. Goodnow, and G. A. Austin, eds. Pp. 247–
         312. New York: Wiley.
Bultena, Gordon L.
  1968   Age-grading in the Social Interaction of an Elderly Male Pop-
         ulation. Journal of Gerontology 25:539–543.
  1974   Structural Effects on the Morale of the Aged: A Comparison
         of Age-segregated and Age-integrated Communities. In Late
         Life: Communities and Environmental Policy. Jaber F. Gubrium,
         ed. Pp. 18–31. Springfield, Ill.: Charles C. Thomas.
Bultena, Gordon L., and Edward A. Powers
  1978   Denial of Aging: Age Identification and Reference Group
         Orientations. Journal of Gerontology 33:748–754.
Bultena, Gordon L., and V. Wood
  1969   The American Retirement Community: Bane or Blessing?
         Journal of Gerontology 24:209–217.

Butler, Robert N.
    1963   The Life Review: An Interpretation of Reminiscence in the
         Aged. Psychiatry 26:65–76.
    1976   Why Survive? New York: Harper and Row.
Byrne, Susan
    1974   Arden, An Adult Community. *In* The Anthropology of Cit-
         ies. George M. Foster and Robert V. Kemper, eds. Pp. 123–152.
         Boston: Little, Brown.
Carp, Frances M.
    1977   Housing and Living Environments of Older People. *In*
         Handbook of Aging and the Social Sciences. Robert H. Binstock
         and Ethel Shanas, eds. Pp. 244–271. New York: Van Nostrand
         Reinhold.
Clark, M. Margaret
    1967   The Anthropology of Aging, A New Area for Studies of
         Culture and Personality. Gerontologist 7:55–64.
Clark, M. Margaret, and Barbara Anderson
    1967   Culture and Aging. Springfield, Ill.: Charles C. Thomas
Clark, M. Margaret, Sharon Kaufman, and Robert C. Pierce
    1976   Explorations of Acculturation: Toward a Model of Ethnic
         Identity. Human Organization 35:231–238.
Clark, M. Margaret, and Christie Kiefer
    1971   Working Paper on Ethnic Identity. Human Development
         Program, University of California San Francisco: mimeo.
Cohen, Yehudi A.
    1971   The Shaping of Men's Minds: Adaptations to Imperatives of
         Culture. *In* Anthropological Perspectives on Education. Murray
         L. Wax, Stanley Diamond, and Fred O. Gearing, eds. Pp. 19–50.
         New York: Basic Books.
Cool, Linda Evers
    1978   Ethnicity and the Aged: "Triple Jeopardy" or Power Re-
         source? Paper presented at the Annual Meeting of the American
         Anthropological Association, Los Angeles, California.
    1979   Ethnicity and Aging: Continuity Through Change for El-
         derly Corsicans. *In* Aging in Culture and Society: Comparative
         Viewpoints and Strategies. Christine L. Fry, ed. New York: J. F.
         Bergin Press.
Cowgill, Donald, and Lowell Holmes, eds.
    1972   Aging and Modernization. New York: Appleton-Century-
         Crofts.

Cuellar, Jose
  1978 El Senior Citizens Club: The Older Mexican-American in the Voluntary Association. *In* Life's Career—Aging: Cultural Variations on Growing Old, Barbara G. Myerhoff and Andrei Simic, eds. Pp. 207–230. Beverly Hills: Sage Publications.
Cumming, Elaine, and David M. Schneider
  1961 Sibling Solidarity: A Property of American Kinship. American Anthropologist 63:498–507.
Davis, Fred
  1961 Deviance Disavowal: The Management of Strained Interaction by the Visibly Handicapped. Social Problems 9:120–132.
  1963 Passage through Crisis. Indianapolis: Bobbs-Merrill.
Dignum, Kirk A.
  1979 A Telephone Communication Network in a Dispersed Community Setting. Paper presented at the Annual Meeting of the Southwestern Anthropological Association, Santa Barbara, California, March 29–31.
Dowd, James J.
  1975 Aging as Exchange: A Preface to Theory. Journal of Gerontology 30:584–594.
Dowd, James J., and Vern L. Bengston
  1978 Aging in Minority Populations: An Examination of the Double Jeopardy Hypothesis. Journal of Gerontology 33:427–436.
Eaton, Joseph
  1952 Controlled Acculturation. American Sociological Review 17:331–340.
Erikson, Erik H.
  1950 Childhood and Society. New York: Norton.
Fischer, C. S., R. M. Jackson, C. A. Steuve, K. Gerson, L. McAllister Jones, and M. Baldassare
  1977 Networks and Places: Social Relations in the Urban Setting. New York: Free Press.
Foner, Anne
  1975 Age in Society: Structure and Change. American Behavioral Scientist 19:144–165.
Frake, Charles O.
  1964 How to Ask for a Drink in Subanum. American Anthropologist 66:6, Part 2:127–132.
Fry, Christine L.
  1977 The Community as a Commodity: The Age-graded Case. Human Organization 36:115–123.

Furth, Hans G.
1966 Thinking without Language. New York: Free Press.
Gans, Herbert J.
1962 The Urban Villagers. New York: Free Press.
Geer, J. H.
1965 The Development of a Scale to Measure Fear. Behavior Research and Therapy 3:45–53.
Geertz, Clifford
1973 Interpretation of Cultures. New York: Basic Books.
Glaser, Barney, and Anselm Strauss
1971 Status Passage. Chicago: Aldine.
Gluckman, Max
1963 Gossip and Scandal. Current Anthropology 4:307–316.
Goffman, Erving
1961 Asylums. Garden City, N.Y.: Doubleday.
1963 Stigma: Notes on the Management of Spoiled Identity. Englewood Cliffs, N.J.: Prentice-Hall.
Goist, Doris
1978 Adaptive Strategies of the Elderly in England and Ohio. Paper presented at the Annual Meeting of the American Anthropological Association, Los Angeles, November.
1979 Age and Identity in Cleveland and Leeds: A Comparative Study. Paper presented at the Annual Meeting of the American Anthropological Association, Cincinnati, Ohio, November.
Groce, Nora
1978 Congenital Deafness on Martha's Vineyard: The Sociolinguistics of a Hereditary Medical Disorder. Paper presented at the Annual Meeting of the American Anthropological Association, Los Angeles, California, November.
Gumperz, John
1962 Types of Linguistic Communities. Anthropological Linguistics 4:14–26.
Hallowell, A. I.
1955 Culture and Experience. New York: Schocken.
Hanks, J. R., and Hanks, L. M.
1948 The Physically Handicapped in Certain Non-Occidental Societies. Journal of Social Issues 4:11–20.
Havighurst, Robert J., Bernice L. Neugarten, and S. S. Tobin
1968 Disengagement and Patterns of Aging. *In* Middle Age and Aging. Bernice L. Neugarten, ed. Pp. 161–172. Chicago: University of Chicago Press.

Hochschild, Arlie
    1973   The Unexpected Community. Englewood Cliffs, N.J.: Prentice-Hall.
Hurlock, Elizabeth
    1967   Adolescent Development. New York: McGraw-Hill.
Huyck, Margaret H.
    1974   Growing Older: Things You Need to Know about Aging. Englewood Cliffs, N.J.: Prentice-Hall.
Hyman, Martin D.
    1971   The Stigma of Stroke. Geriatrics 16:132–141.
Jackson, Jacqueline J.
    1971   The Blacklands of Gerontology. Aging and Human Development 2:156–171.
    1976   Aged Negroes: Their Cultural Departures from Statistical Stereotypes and Rural-Urban Differences. *In* Contemporary Social Gerontology: Significant Developments in the Field of Aging. Bill D. Bell, ed. Pp. 328–334. Springfield, Ill.: Charles C. Thomas.
Jackson, James S., J. D. Bacon, and J. Peterson
    1977–78   Life Satisfaction among Black Urban Elderly. Journal of Aging and Human Development 8:169–179.
Jacobs, Jerry
    1974   Fun City: An Ethnographic Study of a Retirement Community. New York: Holt, Rinehart and Winston.
Jacobs, Leo
    1974   A Deaf Adult Speaks Out. Washington, D.C.: Gallaudet College Press.
Johnson, Colleen
    1979   Interdependence and Aging among Italian-Americans. Journal of Minority Aging 4(1):34–41.
Johnson, Sheila
    1971   Idle Haven: Community Building Among the Working-Class Retired. Berkeley: University of California Press.
Kalish, Richard
    1975   Late Adulthood: Perspectives on Human Development. Monterey, Calif.: Brookes/Cole.
    1977   Death and Dying in a Social Context. *In* Handbook of Aging and the Social Sciences. Robert H. Binstock and Ethel Shanas, eds. Pp. 483–509. New York: Van Nostrand Reinhold.
Kassebaum, Gene G., and Barbara O. Baumann
    1965   Dimensions of the Sick Role in Chronic Illness. Journal of Health and Human Behavior 6:16–27.

Kaufman, Sharon
  1980 A Phenomenological Study of Identity and Aging. Unpublished Ph.D. Dissertation, University of California San Francisco.
Kiefer, Christie W.
  1974 Changing Cultures, Changing Lives. San Francisco: Jossey-Bass.
Kirkpatrick, Clifford, and Charles Hobart
  1954 Disagreement, Disagreement Estimate, and Non-empathetic Imputations for Intimacy Groups Varying from Favorite Date to Married. American Sociological Review 19:10–19.
Kleemeier, R. W.
  1954 Moosehaven: Congregate Living in a Community of the Retired. American Journal of Sociology 59:347–351.
Lee, Dorothy
  1959 Freedom and Culture. Englewood Cliffs, N.J.: Prentice-Hall.
Levine, Edna A.
  1958 Psychological Aspects and Problems of Early Profound Deafness. American Annals of the Deaf 103:72–95.
Lipman, Aaron
  1970 Prestige of the Aged in Portugal: Realistic Appraisal and Ritualistic Deference. Aging and Human Development 1:127–136.
Lipman, Aaron, and R. S. Sterne
  1969 Aging in the United States: Ascription of a Terminal Sick Role. Sociology and Social Research 53:194–203.
Lofland, J.
  1968 The Youth Ghetto. Journal of Higher Education 39:121–143.
Lowenthal, Marjorie F., and Betsy Robinson
  1977 Social Networks and Isolation. *In* Handbook of Aging and the Social Sciences. Robert H. Binstock and Ethel Shanas, eds. Pp. 432–456. New York: Van Nostrand Reinhold.
Lowenthal, Marjorie F., Majda Thurnher, and David Chiriboga
  1975 Four Stages of Life. San Francisco: Jossey-Bass.
Lozier, John, and Ronald Althouse
  1974 Social Enforcement of Behavior toward Elders in an Appalachian Mountain Settlement. Gerontologist 14:69–80.
McCullers, Carson
  1940 The Heart Is a Lonely Hunter. Boston: Houghton Mifflin.
McDaniel, James W.
  1969 Physical Disability and Human Behavior. New York: Pergamon Press.

McNeill, David
  1965   The Capacity for Language Acquisition. *In* Research on Behavioral Aspects of Deafness. Washington, D.C.: Vocational Rehabilitation Administration, USDHEW.
Maxwell, Robert J., and Philip Silverman
  1970   Information and Esteem: Cultural Considerations in the Treatment of the Aged. Aging and Human Development 1:361–392.
  1978   The Nature of Deference. Current Anthropology 19:151.
Mayer, Philip, and Iona Mayer
  1970   Socialization by Peers: The Youth Organization of Red Xhosa. *In* Socialization: The Approach from Social Anthropology. Philip Mayer, ed. Pp. 159–189. London: Tavistock.
Mead, George Herbert
  1934   Mind, Self, and Society. Chicago: University of Chicago Press.
Mead, Margaret
  1970   Culture and Commitment: A Study of the Generation Gap. New York: Natural History Press.
Meadow, Kathryn P.
  1968   Parental Response to the Medical Ambiguities of Deafness. Journal of Health and Social Behavior 9:299–309.
  1972   Sociolinguistics, Sign Language, and the Deaf Subculture. *In* Psycholinguistics and Total Communication: The State of the Art. Terry O'Rourke, ed. Pp. 19–33. Washington, D.C.: American Annals of the Deaf.
  1974   The Quiet Worlds of Deafness—A Sociological Description of the Deaf Subculture. Faculty Workshop, California State University, Hayward, October 15. Mimeo.
  1975   The Development of Deaf Children. *In* Review of Child Development Research. E. Mavis Hetherington, ed. Pp. 441–508. Chicago: University of Chicago Press.
  1976   Personal and Social Development of Deaf Persons. *In* Psychology of Deafness for Rehabilitation Counselors. B. Bolton, ed. Baltimore. University Park Press.
Miller, D.
  1963   The Study of Social Relationships: Situation, Identity, and Social Interaction. *In* Psychology: The Study of a Science. S. Koch, ed. Pp. 639–737. New York: McGraw-Hill.
Mithun, Jacqueline
  1973   Cooperation and Solidarity as Survival Necessities in a Black Urban Community. Urban Anthropology 2:25–34.

Moore, Sally Falk
  1978 Old Age in a Life-Term Social Arena: Some Chagga of Kilimanjaro in 1974. *In* Life's Career—Aging: Cultural Variations on Growing Old. Barbara G. Myerhoff and Andrei Simic, eds. Pp. 23–76. Beverly Hills: Sage Publications.
Myerhoff, Barbara G.
  1978a Number Our Days. New York: Dutton.
  1978b A Symbol Perfected in Death: Continuity and Ritual in the Life and Death of an Elderly Jew. *In* Life's Career—Aging: Cultural Variations on Growing Old. Barbara G. Myerhoff and Andrei Simic, eds. Pp. 163–206. Beverly Hills: Sage Publications.
Neugarten, Bernice
  1972 Personality and the Aging Process. Gerontologist 12:9–15.
  1974 Age Groups in American Society and the Rise of the Young-Old. Annals of the American Academy of Science 9:187–198.
Neugarten, Bernice, and Gunhild O. Hagestad
  1977 Age and the Life Course. *In* Handbook of Aging and the Social Sciences. Robert H. Binstock and Ethel Shanas, eds. Pp. 35–55. New York: Van Nostrand Reinhold.
Newman, Kathy
  1974 Discussants' Comments in Symposium on Culture and Language in the Deaf Community. Annual Meeting of the American Anthropological Association, Mexico City, November.
O'Nell, C. W.
  1972 Aging in a Zapotec Community. Human Development 15:294–309.
Padden, Carol, and Harry Markowicz
  1975 Cultural Conflict between Hearing and Deaf Communities. Washington, D.C.: Gallaudet College, mimeo.
Parsons, Talcott, and Renee Fox
  1958 Illness, Therapy, and the Modern Urban American Family. *In* Patients, Physicians, and Illness. E. Gartly Jaco, ed. Pp. 234–245. Glencoe, Ill.: Free Press.
Rainer, John D., K. Altschuler, and F. J. Kallman
  1963 Family and Mental Health Problems in a Deaf Population. New York: Columbia University, New York State Psychiatric Institute.
Redfield, Robert
  1955 The Little Community. Chicago: University of Chicago Press.

Riley, Matilda W., Anne Foner, and Associates
  1968   Aging and Society: Vol. 1, An Inventory of Research Findings. New York: Russell Sage.
Rosow, Irving
  1967   Social Integration of the Aged. New York: Free Press.
  1970   Old People: Their Friends and Neighbors. *In* Aging in a Contemporary Society. Ethel Shanas, ed. Pp. 57–67. Beverly Hills: Sage Publications.
  1973   The Social Context of the Aging Self. Gerontologist 13:82–87.
  1974   Socialization to Old Age. Berkeley: University of California Press.
Ross, Jennie-Keith
  1975   Social Borders: Definitions of Diversity. Current Anthropology 16:53–72.
  1977   Old People, New Lives: Community Creation in a Retirement Residence. Chicago: University of Chicago Press.
Schein, Jerome
  1968   The Deaf Community. Washington, D.C.: Gallaudet College Press.
Schein, Jerome, and Marcus T. Delk
  1974   The Deaf Population of the United States. Silver Springs, Md.: National Association of the Deaf.
Schlesinger, Hilde S.
  1972   Responsiveness of the Environment—Residential School Living. *In* Inservice Training of Afterclass Staff in Residential Schools for Deaf Children. D. W. Naiman, ed. New York: Deafness Research and Training Center, New York University.
Schlesinger, Hilde S., and Kathryn P. Meadow
  1972   Sound and Sign. Berkeley: University of California Press.
Seguin, M.
  1973   Opportunity for Peer Socialization in a Retirement Community. Gerontologist 13:203–214.
Sheehy, Gail
  1976   Passages. New York: Dutton.
Sherman, Susan
  1975   Patterns of Contact for Residents of Age-segregated and Age-integrated Housing. Journal of Gerontology 30:103–107.
Sigerist, Henry
  1943   Civilization and Disease. Chicago: University of Chicago Press.

Simic, Andrei
  1978 Introduction: Aging and the Aged in Cultural Perspective. *In* Life's Career—Aging: Cultural Variations on Growing Old. Barbara G. Myerhoff and Andrei Simic, eds. Pp. 1–22. Beverly Hills: Sage Publications.
Simmons, Leo
  1945 The Role of the Aged in Primitive Society. New Haven: Yale University Press.
Singlemann, Peter
  1972 Exchange as Symbolic Interaction: Convergences between Two Theoretical Perspectives. American Sociological Review 37:414–424.
Snyder, Peter Z.
  1973 Social Interaction Patterns and Relative Urban Success: The Denver Navajo. Urban Anthropology 2:1–24.
Spiro, Melford
  1965 Children of the Kibbutz. New York: Schocken.
Spradley, Thomas S., and James P. Spradley
  1978 Deaf Like Me. New York: Random House.
Stack, Carol
  1974 All Our Kin: Strategies for Survival in a Black Community. New York: Harper and Row.
Stein, Maurice R.
  1960 The Eclipse of Community. New York: Harper and Row.
Stokoe, William C.
  1960 Sign Language Structure: An Outline of the Visual Communication Systems of the American Deaf. Buffalo, N.Y.: Occasional Papers #8, University of Buffalo.
Strauss, Anselm L.
  1975 Chronic Illness and the Quality of Life. St. Louis, Mo.: C. V. Mosby.
Streib, Gordon F.
  1965 Are the Aged a Minority Group? *In* Applied Sociology. A. W. Gouldner and S. M. Miller, eds. Pp. 311–328. Glencoe, Ill.: Free Press.
  1970 Old Age and the Family: Facts and Forecasts. *In* Aging in Contemporary Society. Ethel Shanas, ed. Pp. 25–39. Beverly Hills: Sage Publications.
Sussman, Marvin B.
  1977 The Family Life of Old People. *In* Handbook of Aging and the Social Sciences. Robert H. Binstock and Ethel Shanas, eds. Pp. 218–243.

Teaff, Joseph D., M. Powell Lawton, Lucille Nahemow, and Diane
Carlson
1978   Impact of Age-Integration on the Well-being of Elderly Tenants in Public Housing. Journal of Gerontology 33:126–133.

Turner, Victor
1969   The Ritual Process. Ithaca, N.Y.: Cornell University Press.

Vernon, McKay, and B. Makowsky
1969   Deafness and Minority Group Dynamics. The Deaf American, July/August: 3–6.

Wallace, Anthony F. C.
1967   Identity Processes in Personality and in Culture. *In* Cognition, Personality, and Clinical Psychology. Richard Jessor and
Seymour Feshbach, eds. Pp. 62–89. San Francisco: Jossey-Bass.

Ward, Russell A.
1977   The Impact of Subjective Age and Stigma on Older Persons.
Journal of Gerontology 32:227–232.

Watson, Wilbur H., and Maxwell, Robert J.
1977   Human Aging and Dying: A Study in Sociocultural Gerontology. New York: St. Martins Press.

Weiss, Lawrence J.
1979   Intimacy and Adaptation. *In* Sexuality in the Later Years:
Roles and Behavior. Ruth Weg, ed. Menlo Park, Calif.: Addison-
Wesley Publishing Co.

Whorf, Benjamin Lee
1956   Language, Thought, and Reality: Selected Writings of Benjamin Lee Whorf. J. B. Carroll, ed. Cambridge, Mass., and New
York: Technological Press of MIT and John Wiley.

Wilensky, Harold L.
1961   Life Cycle, Work Situation, and Participation in Formal Associations. *In* Aging and Leisure. Robert W. Kleemeier, ed. Pp.
213–242. New York: Oxford University Press.

Williams, Gerry C.
1979   Warriors No More: A Study of the Indian Elderly. *In* Aging
in Culture and Society: Comparative Viewpoints and Strategies.
Christine L. Fry, ed. New York: J. F. Bergin Press.

Wright, Beatrice
1960   Physical Disability: A Psychological Approach. New York:
Harper and Row.

Yambert, Gay Becker, and Roger Van Craeynest
1975   Sign Language and Social Networks: Grapevine Communication in the Deaf Community. Paper presented at the Annual

Meeting of the Southwestern Anthropological Association, San Francisco, March.

Yarrow, Leon J.
1964 Separation from Parents during Early Childhood. *In* Review of Child Development Research. Martin L. Hoffman and Lois W. Hoffman, eds. Pp. 89–136. New York: Russell Sage Foundation.

Zahn, M. A.
1973 Incapacity, Impotence, and Invisible Impairments: Their Effects upon Interpersonal Relations. Journal of Health and Human Behavior 14:115–123.

Index

Designer: Jim Mennick
Compositor: G & S Typesetters
Printer: Vail-Ballou
Binder: Vail-Ballou
Text: VIP Palatino
Display: Baker Danmark
Cloth: Holliston Roxite B 51507